WINSLOW HOMER

The Nature and Rhythm of Life

from the
Arkell Museum
at Canajoharie

WINSLOW HOMER

The Nature and Rhythm of Life
from the
Arkell Museum
at Canajoharie

DIANE E. FORSBERG
and MARTHA HOPPIN

with essays by
SARAH BURNS
and DAVID TATHAM

Catalogue and Exhibition Organized by the Arkell Museum at Canajoharie, New York
For the Fenimore Art Museum, Cooperstown, New York

Winslow Homer: *The Nature and Rhythm of Life from the Arkell Museum at Canajoharie*

By Diane E. Forsberg and Martha Hoppin
with essays by Sarah Burns and David Tatham

Editor: Martha Hoppin

Published in conjunction with the exhibition
*Winslow Homer: The Nature and Rhythm of Life
from the Arkell Museum at Canajoharie*
Organized by the Arkell Museum at Canajoharie
At the Fenimore Art Museum, Cooperstown, New York
June 6–August 24, 2014
At the Arkell Museum, Canajoharie, New York
September 2, 2014–January 4, 2015

Copyedited by Jamie Nan Thaman
Designed and Produced by Nadeau Design Associates
Printed by Canfield & Tack, Rochester, New York

Arkell Museum at Canajoharie, www.arkellmuseum.org
Fenimore Art Museum, www.fenimoreartmuseum.org

Exhibition and Catalogue Sponsors:
The Morgan McReynolds Group at Morgan Stanley
Erna Morgan McReynolds, Financial Advisor
Morgan Stanley Smith Barney LLC. Member SIPC

State of the Arts

NYSCA

This exhibition is made possible by the
New York State Council on the Arts
with the support of Governor Andrew Cuomo
and the New York State Legislature.

First published in 2014 by the Fenimore Art Museum
Lake Road—P.O. Box 800, Cooperstown, NY 13326
ISBN: 978-0-917334-45-0

Cover: (Detail) Winslow Homer,
Watching the Breakers—A High Sea, 1896 (see cat. 22)

Title Page: (Detail) Winslow Homer,
Moonlight, 1874 (see cat. 8)

Contents: (Detail) Winslow Homer,
Sailing Out of Gloucester, ca. 1880 (see cat. 15)

CONTENTS

FOREWORD AND ACKNOWLEDGMENTS

THIS PROJECT is the culmination of several years of developing a close working relationship between the Fenimore Art Museum and the Arkell Museum. The outstanding collection of American art at the Arkell has been well-known for decades, and has graced the walls of both of our museums in a number of popular exhibitions over the years. Of particular note in the Arkell's collection are, of course, the twenty-one works by Winslow Homer. It has been a great pleasure to work together this year to further document and share this incomparable collection of masterworks.

We have many people to thank for their contributions to this project. Much of the work was made possible by a generous grant from the New York State Council on the Arts with the support of Governor Andrew Cuomo and the New York State Legislature. We are grateful for the hard work and careful scholarship of the catalogue's authors, Sarah Burns, Diane Forsberg, Martha Hoppin, and David Tatham. As always, Richard Nadeau has contributed a stunning design for the volume.

We also extend our thanks to the following: The Williamstown Art Conservation Center, for the examination of watercolors and attendant reports by Leslie Paisley and photography by Matthew Hamilton; the Archives of American Art, Smithsonian Institution, Washington, D.C., which assisted the Arkell Museum for many years by providing microfilm and direct access to Canajoharie Art Gallery correspondence and Macbeth Gallery records; the Stockman Family Foundation for its many years of support of the collection and its recent grant to examine and re-mat the Winslow Homer watercolors; Stephanie Buck, Librarian/Archivist, Cape Ann Museum, Gloucester, Massachusetts; Catherine Petersen, Library Director, Crystal Bridges Museum of American Art; Suzan Friedlander, Collections Manager for the Arkell Museum, for her valuable assistance in this project; the scholarship of Lloyd Goodrich, edited and expanded by Abigail Booth Gerdts, and published as *Record of Works by Winslow Homer*, which has been vital to all aspects of our project; and our outside lenders, Cheryl A. Chase and Stuart Bear, and the Metropolitan Museum of Art.

Without the support of the respective Boards of Trustees of the Arkell Museum and the Fenimore Art Museum this collaboration would not have been possible. Their enthusiasm for this joint project has been the major component of its success. Of course, none of this would have been possible had it not been for the vision and commitment of Bartlett Arkell, who assembled this remarkable collection and gave it to the people of our region. We are pleased and proud to carry on the legacy that he established.

Paul S. D'Ambrosio
President and CEO, Fenimore Art Museum

Diane E. Forsberg
Museum Director and Chief Curator, Arkell Museum at Canajoharie

(Detail) Winslow Homer, **Sponge Fishing, Bahamas**, ca. 1885 (see cat. 20)

Bartlett Arkell and the Soul-Inspiring Work of Winslow Homer
Diane E. Forsberg

1. Robert Brackman (1898–1980)
Portrait of Bartlett Arkell (1862–1946), 1939
Oil on canvas, 40¼ x 36 inches.
Arkell Museum at Canajoharie,
Gift of Bartlett Arkell, 1944

opposite top
2. Photographer unknown
Original Arkell Gallery at Canajoharie, ca. 1935
Photograph. Arkell Museum at Canajoharie.
Works by Winslow Homer on display include
Watching the Breakers—A High Sea at right
and watercolors on the back wall.

opposite bottom.
3. Winslow Homer (1836–1910)
On the Beach, ca. 1869
Oil on canvas, 15 x 24½ inches.
Arkell Museum at Canajoharie,
Gift of Bartlett Arkell, 1932. Cat. no. 2

BARTLETT ARKELL began collecting American art
in the 1920s, but it was the art of Winslow Homer
that ultimately captured his attention in 1931
and became his enduring inspiration (fig. 1). His
collecting of Homers commenced seven years
after he donated paintings by Robert Henri and
George Bellows to the Canajoharie Library, and
four years after the adjoining gallery first opened
to the public. Both the library (1924) and the art
gallery (1927), complete with copies of European
art alongside original works by leading American
artists (fig. 2), were presented by Arkell as gifts to
his hometown—the Village of Canajoharie.

Bartlett Arkell was raised in this upstate New
York village, where his father was a successful
businessman and newspaper publisher. After
graduating from Yale University, Bartlett worked
with his father at Arkell & Smiths in Canajoharie,
and then ventured to New York City to work for
his older brother, William J. Arkell, who published
Judge and *Leslie's Weekly* magazines. Bartlett
started a couple of his own businesses before he
founded his most successful company in 1889—
the Imperial Packing Company, which was soon
renamed the Beech-Nut Packaging Company.[1]
Beech-Nut primarily packaged food in vacuum-
packed glass jars, but chewing gum, introduced in
1910, turned out to be the company's best-selling
product during the Great Depression. Bartlett's
achievements in business provided him with
enough money during this difficult financial era
to purchase art for his personal collection and for
the people of Canajoharie.

Arkell began the Canajoharie Art Gallery's
Winslow Homer collection with two 1873 Gloucester watercolors, *The See-Saw* and *Boy on Rocks*.
Fifteen years later, after Arkell had purchased an
additional fifteen Homer works for the gallery, he
wrote to Lloyd Goodrich at the Whitney Museum
of American Art expressing how deeply he was

moved by Homer's oil painting *On the Beach*, ca. 1869 (fig. 3), which he had acquired in 1932: "This picture of Winslow Homer has done more to exalt my spirit and put me in another world than all the other pictures that I have put together. I call it soul inspiring. . . . The first time I saw it I couldn't sleep at all that night and the same thing happened to the young lady in the Macbeth Gallery. There must be something in this picture that one does not find very frequently in any art."[2]

It is remarkable that Arkell's "soul inspiring" Homer painting was once part of a larger work criticized as a "horror."[3] Possibly as a result of that criticism, *On the Beach* was cut from the original and altered by Homer, and remained unsold during his lifetime. During the time Bartlett Arkell was purchasing works by Homer, the public and critics had almost universal praise for the work of this American artist.

Arkell obtained twenty-five Homer works through the Macbeth Gallery in New York City between 1931 and 1945. Most works were shipped directly to the Canajoharie Library Gallery and a few went to his residence in New York City. In January 1936, Arkell wrote about sending Homer's *Watching the Breakers—A High Sea*, 1896, and an Inness painting to the gallery "during the summer months. I think it is a fair proposition, as I am really dividing the pleasure and paying the cost. In this respect I am not a good New Dealer, for I

find as a rule those who preach most, practice least."[4] By the mid-1930s, many business leaders were not supporters of the Second New Deal, which they believed was handing out too much federal money while encouraging changes that were unfavorable to their businesses. Arkell was a Republican who felt it was his obligation, not the government's, to provide for his workers and the people of Canajoharie. This is why he sponsored so many of the town's necessities and niceties, including flowers hanging from lampposts, a traffic light, and the library and art gallery.

There was in Arkell's mind flexibility as to where the paintings would be hung after he gave them to the Canajoharie Gallery. Some of the paintings Arkell collected were so beloved by him that he would bring them to his home for long periods of time. This was the case with *On the Beach*, and he noted in his 1944 letter to Goodrich that this painting "now hangs in my doorway which I see every time I pass into the house and from the house."

4. Charles Lowell Homer (1881–1955)
Interior of Homer's Studio, 100th birthday exhibition, 1936
Photograph. Bowdoin College Museum of Art, Brunswick, Maine, Gift of the Homer Family, Homer Memorabilia 26.7. *Woman on the Beach, Marshfield* is right of the fireplace.

Bartlett Arkell's acquisitions for the Canajoharie Gallery span Winslow Homer's career, with one notable exception: there are no Adirondack subjects of fishing or hunting. According to Macbeth Gallery sales records, Arkell did buy a Homer painting called *Trout* in August 1940, which he gave to Dudley Clarke (Duckie) Corkran of the Orvis Fishing Rod Company, located in Manchester, Vermont, where the Arkells had a summer home.

Most of the Homer paintings Arkell purchased for Canajoharie depict scenes by the ocean or on a farm. Arkell was always attracted to farmland views, and he collected many landscapes by George Inness and others that reminded him of the agricultural landscape near his upstate New York factories. Beech-Nut packaged bacon, jam, and other food products in its early years, before gum and baby food, and his company promoted the idea of "clean bright Beech-Nut plants nestled in the hills of the Mohawk Valley,"[5] alongside farms and far away from the less pristine city.

The Homer farm subjects purchased by Arkell include *Feeding the Chickens*, *The Pumpkin Patch*, *Little Shepherdess*, and *Shepherdess and Sheep*.[6] *The Rooster*, the last Homer painting purchased for the Canajoharie Gallery (in 1945), went directly to the gallery. *Feeding the Chickens*, listed by Macbeth Gallery as the "Earliest Known oil: date determined by apparent age of Arthur B. Homer, the boy in the picture,"[7] was so treasured by Bartlett's wife, Louise, that she kept it in her home throughout her life.

Bartlett Arkell may have been aware that some of the Homer farm subjects in his collection were created at Houghton Farm near Mountainville, New York, in 1878 and 1879. Arkell was a teenager attending Williston Academy in Easthampton, Massachusetts, when Homer was painting at Houghton Farm. Henry E. Alvord, an instructor at the Academy, left during Arkell's time there to become general manager of Houghton Farm and its scientific studies to modernize agriculture.[8]

Arkell purchased farm views by many artists, but almost all of his ocean views were painted by Winslow Homer. The ocean-themed works trace Homer's career, from his early interest in summer seaside subjects at Long Branch, New Jersey—as seen in *On the Beach*—to his fascination with the ocean waves at Prout's Neck, Maine. The Arkell collection also includes several masterful and pioneering watercolors from oceanside locations at Gloucester, Massachusetts, and Cullercoats, England.

Winslow Homer was born in 1836 and died in 1910. The 100th anniversary of his birth sparked exhibitions at major museums and commercial galleries. At least eight of the works now in the Arkell collection were featured in these celebratory events. By 1936, Arkell owned six Winslow Homer works. The *Century Loan Exhibition as a Memorial to Winslow Homer*, held in the artist's studio at Prout's Neck in June 1936, included one work from Arkell's collection, but four other works listed in the exhibition catalogue would eventually be purchased by Arkell (fig. 4). *Watching the Breakers—A High Sea* was selected from the Canajoharie collection by Lloyd Goodrich for the *Centenary Exhibition* at the Whitney Museum of American Art, and then this painting, along with a Homer watercolor owned by Arkell, traveled to the Carnegie Institute for its *Centenary Exhibition of Works of Winslow Homer*.

Macbeth Gallery celebrated the centennial by exhibiting seventy-six Homer works in its *Introduction to Winslow Homer*. Arkell already owned one of the watercolors in the Macbeth show and, over time, purchased four other works from the exhibition. Macbeth Gallery was, in fact, Bartlett Arkell's introduction to Winslow Homer, and he relied on the gallery's Robert Macbeth (1884–1940) and Robert McIntyre (1885–1965) to guide and secure his collection of works by Homer. That guidance resulted in a collection that extends over Winslow Homer's career and includes some of his best-known works. Macbeth Gallery encouraged Arkell's interest in acquiring art by constantly bringing new works to his attention. On December 6, 1939, Arkell acknowledged the delivery of a William Merritt Chase painting and also noted: "Thanks for sending along the Homer water colors. I shall be delighted to look upon them again as I drink my morning orange juice."[9] Bartlett Arkell

truly enjoyed his role as collector and integrated art into his daily life, but he was just as enthusiastic about sharing his appreciation of art with the people who worked for his companies and lived in his hometown. It was Arkell's intent that this collection be on display in the gallery he built in Canajoharie. The few Homer works that remained in his personal collection at the time of his death in 1946 have been reunited with the Canajoharie collection for this publication and exhibition.

NOTES

1. "Beech-Nut," *Fortune* 14, no. 5 (November 1936): 92, includes the following information and quotation often shared by the company: The Imperial Packaging Company was named after the hotel in New York City where Bartlett Arkell had lived while working at his brother's publishing company. A year later, the name changed to Beech-Nut at the suggestion of a family friend, a Saratoga casino owner and art connoisseur, who thought that "Imperial was an undemocratic name for a ham."

2. Letter from Bartlett Arkell to Lloyd Goodrich, Whitney Museum of American Art, New York, 1944, carbon copy in Arkell Museum curatorial files.

3. "Fine Arts: The Winter Exhibition of the National Academy of Design," *New York Evening Mail*, November 6, 1869, quoted in Margaret C. Conrads, *Winslow Homer and the Critics: Forging a National Art in the 1870s* (Princeton, N.J.: Princeton University Press, in association with the Nelson-Atkins Museum of Art, 2001), 20.

4. Letter from Bartlett Arkell, New York, N.Y., to Frank Barbour, Canajoharie, N.Y., January 17, 1936, Arkell Museum curatorial files.

5. Beech-Nut company letter from Bartlett's son, William C. Arkell, to the New York State Division of Commerce, 1944, Arkell Museum curatorial files.

6. Unbeknown to Bartlett Arkell, or anyone else until 1969, *Shepherdess and Sheep* included another farm scene, *Girl at the Fence*, hidden underneath on the same stretcher.

7. *An Introduction to Homer* (New York: Macbeth Gallery, December 15, 1936–January 18, 1937). The painting was listed a few months earlier with the words "This is probably Homer's first work in oil" in the catalogue *Prout's Neck Century Loan Exhibition as a Memorial to Winslow Homer by the Prout's Neck Association*, 1936. A copy of the catalogue has handwritten next to the entry "did not come" (probably by the person arranging the return of artwork to owners). Macbeth Gallery records, 1838–1968, bulk 1892–1953, Archives of American Art, Smithsonian Institution, Box 1, folder 10.

8. *Agricultural Review and Industrial Monthly* 1, no. 2 (1882): 258.

9. Letter from Bartlett Arkell to Macbeth Gallery, December 6, 1939, Arkell Museum curatorial files. *Homework*, purchased for the Canajoharie Art Gallery on December 17, 1939, may have been one of the watercolors he was reviewing over orange juice.

THE MAN AND THE MOON

Sarah Burns

IN THE EVER-EXPANDING bibliography of writings on Winslow Homer, there is a set of key words used over and over again, in combinations that over time have established lasting ideas about the artist and his work. While the emphasis may shift from one era to the next, the constants remain. Such terms define Homer as a realist: a master of observation, impersonal and unsentimental in his scrutiny of the world before him. Those attributes in turn qualify Homer as a seminal modern master, the arc of his career tracing a path from the keen-eyed depiction of modern life to a heroic engagement with elemental nature, conveyed in an austere visual language that ultimately borders on abstraction. There are many more nuances to the story than my broad strokes convey. Yet by and large, the outlines are correct, however we choose to fill them in. Look at almost any American art history syllabus: Homer, the quintessential realist, stands at the opposite extreme from that other-worldly romantic, Albert Pinkham Ryder.

And yet when we look upon Homer's 1874 watercolor *Moonlight* (fig. 5), the adjective *realist* may be the last word to come to mind as we fall under its spell. The design is simple: a strip of sand, a couple in silhouette, a full silvery moon shining over a tranquil sea, and on the distant horizon a lone schooner. Close together but not touching, the man and woman, their shadows black behind them, gaze out at the ocean, where the swell of a rising wave punctuates the shimmering watery expanse with a slash of deepest teal. On the right, a breaker flings up a spray of foam. In the foreground straggle inky seaweed tendrils, echoed above by filmy strands of cloud. Given that the artist had begun seriously working in watercolor only the previous year, *Moonlight* is impressive even from a strictly technical point of view, its bold swathes of paint and refined tonal gradations suggesting a sure hand.

Murky below, suffused with heavenly radiance above, Homer's watercolor is an intensely romantic painting, radiating that aura of enchantment we associate with moonlit summer nights. In Homer's oeuvre, the subject is in fact quite rare. As an illustrator, he drew several night scenes in black and white, but the 1874 watercolor was the first moonlit landscape, or oceanscape, of his painting career.

Moonlight was the product of Homer's sojourn in East Hampton, Long Island, where he traveled with his artist friend Enoch Wood Perry during the summer of 1874. How long they stayed there is uncertain, but the *Evening Post* reported in late October that "Winslow Homer has been revelling among the natives of East Hampton, and brings back as the fruits of his Summer labor, many capital paintings of rustic life."[1] Perry later recalled that he and Homer had shared a two-room cabin on the ocean beach there.[2] *Moonlight* would thus have been the result of direct observation, augmented, no doubt, by a little imagination. Indeed, we can gauge just when Homer might have studied the effects of bright moonlight on water and land:

that summer, the moon was at its fullest on July 28 and August 27.[3]

The other moonlight scene from that summer is the full-page illustration *Flirting on the Sea-Shore and on the Meadow* (fig. 6), published in the September 19 issue of *Harper's Weekly*. In the bottom register, two barefoot farm boys sprawl in a sunny meadow, elbows propped, as they gaze raptly at a little country girl. A pair of ducks parading with several ducklings playfully hints at the eventual outcome of such rustic affections. In the top register, the mood is far more solemn. A grown couple reposes on the moonlit sand. The woman, back to the viewer, sports a voluminous sash and a rustic poke bonnet that conceals her face as she leans toward her companion, a bearded fisherman.[4] Although they seem to be conversing, he gazes absently elsewhere; if this be flirtation, it is uncommonly grave. In the sky at right glows the full moon, lighting up the water and the spray of sea foam splashing up onto the shore. Behind them on the left we see the silhouettes of a windmill and several houses, signs of specific locality missing from the more generalized *Moonlight*.[5]

What drew Homer to moonlight? Aside from the fact that the subject of lovers by the nighttime sea is palpably romantic, the painting is Romantic in a larger sense as well. It harks back to the early nineteenth century, when artists began to project their sensations of cosmic awe

and spiritual longing into landscape paintings imbued with mystery and profound feeling. Homer's connections to such romantic wonderment may have been direct. Born in Boston, he grew up in Cambridge, Massachusetts, where the painter Washington Allston was a mythic figure, both during and long after his lifetime. The beautiful *Moonlight* of 1819 (fig. 7) embodies Allston's

opposite
5. Winslow Homer (1836–1910)
Moonlight, 1874
Watercolor over graphite on wove paper,
13 7/8 x 20 11/16 inches. Arkell Museum at Canajoharie,
Gift of Bartlett Arkell, 1941. Cat. no. 8

above
6. Winslow Homer (1836–1910)
Flirting on the Sea-Shore and on the Meadow
Harper's Weekly, September 19, 1874.
Wood engraving, 9 1/4 x 13 5/8 inches.
Museum of Fine Arts, Boston,
Gift of Edward Jackson Holmes, 30.913

left
7. Washington Allston (1779–1843)
Moonlight, 1819
Oil on canvas, 25 1/8 x 35 3/4 inches.
Museum of Fine Arts, Boston,
William Sturgis Bigelow Collection, 21.1429

romantic vision of the world as a place of enchantment and infinite harmony, melding even the smallest grain of sand with the unimaginable vastness of the Creator's universe.[6] The design underscores that idea: the moon's reflection in the still waters creates a vertical axis that links the silhouetted foreground figures with the celestial orb so far above.

Whether Homer ever saw this painting, which was in the collection of Dr. Henry Jacob Bigelow, must remain a matter of pure conjecture. However, Allston's paintings were well known in the artist community. In *Book of the Artists*, Henry T. Tuckerman made that clear, even mentioning *Moonlit Landscape* [*Moonlight*] in his discussion of Allston's work and influence. Of course, there are many other possible precedents: the dreamy moonlit scenes of Thomas Cole, for example, or of the French Barbizon painters, avidly collected in Boston. Of the latter group, Jean-François Millet in particular comes to mind; in his art, moonlight can transmute the humblest sheepfold into the vision of a strange and magical world.[7] But the point is not so much to zero in on a source as to suggest what Homer and his romantic forerunners might have in common. Like Allston's, the anonymous figures in Homer's *Moonlight* are poised at the brink of infinity; they look out over the trackless ocean and immeasurable nocturnal sky, all part of some cosmic harmony—moon and each tiny grain of sand alike.

But to be a Romantic was not simply a matter of rapt idealism. The Romantic age was an era of ardent scientific enthusiasm and curiosity. It propelled a great surge of experiment, discovery, and invention that inspired creativity in all media. As the century unfolded, new and disquieting discoveries—notably Charles Darwin's—made the reconciliation of traditional beliefs and rational science increasingly problematic. But for some, at least, the solution lay in a new marriage of science and religion that justified the scientific understanding of nature and the universe as but another way to seek and find God. That was the argument systematically laid out by George Chaplin Child in *The Great Architect: Benedicite; Illustrations of the Power, Wisdom, and Goodness of God, as Manifested in His Works*. Homer owned the 1871 edition (there were thirteen in all) and kept it all his life. Clearly, he valued Child's worldview.[8]

One chapter dedicated to the moon exemplifies the delicate balance of poetry, spirituality, and empirical analysis that Child sought to maintain in this magisterial tome. His vision of the moon might have come from the pen of the dreamiest romantic: "Floating in the clear sky, or poised among the fleecy, tinted clouds, silvering the water or piercing through the trees—in every phase and aspect it is beautiful. Like an enchanter it casts the charm of picturesqueness over the meanest objects, and masses which look hard and ugly in the garish light of the Sun mellow into beauty when touched by the power of the moonbeam." What followed this poetic flight, though, was a meticulously detailed scientific analysis of the moon's place and function in the solar system and in relation to the earth that receives its light. Child laid particular emphasis on the moon's crucial role in upholding the "balance" of the solar system. "We know," he asserted, "that it was created by Our Father 'to rule the night,' and in other ways to shed blessings on his children."[9]

For an artist of Homer's sensibility, Child's treatise affirmed what he already believed and practiced in his art. Homer always insisted that his art was based in nature, the ultimate source of truth. *Moonlight* is no exception. For all its poetic beauty, the painting clearly exhibits the artist's close study of the moon's transforming effects on the colors and tones of sky, water, and in particular earth. Under the moon's blue rays, the sand—pale buff in the daytime—is a shadowy brown, subtly tinted with hints of rust and violet. Etched with a filigree of spume, the wave curling onto the shore and sending up a spray of lacy foam seems likewise the result of keen and prolonged scrutiny. Yet at the same time, the entire scene, down to its anonymous figures, is suffused with mystery. Homer seems to have struck just such a balance as Child did in his exposition on the lunar orb. There is enchantment, and there is also painstaking analysis. There is a sense of

8. Thomas Charles Farrer (1839–1891)
Twilight, ca. 1864
Oil on academy board, 8 x 4⅞ inches.
Museum of Fine Arts, Boston,
James E. Neill Memorial Fund, 1996.195

cosmic oneness and harmony, and at the same time a visible effort to capture the exact effect of the moment. Realism here meshes seamlessly with romantic feeling.

Enfolded within Homer's sublimely romantic lunar night, there is, of course, a different sort of romance, a more earthly affair. What might have prompted the artist's excursion into this land of moonlit love? He had any number of precedents on which to draw. The vision of love (or romantic longing, regret, and nostalgia) in the moonlight was a staple in poetry, from the well-known lyrics of Edgar Allan Poe to the most forgettable ephemera. In "Annabel Lee," Poe's narrator recalls his long-ago romance in a "kingdom by the sea," where his fragile maiden, struck down by a chill wind, now lies in a sepulcher on the shore. Night after night, the bereaved lover comes to that place to lay himself down beside her: "For the moon never beams, without bringing me dreams / Of the beautiful Annabel Lee." At the other end of the

spectrum, consider "Discovery of Madeira" by the English versifier William Lisle Bowles: "Woman and man, by vows sincere betrothed, / Heard but the voice of Nature. The still moon / Arose—they saw it not—cheek was to cheek / Inclined, and unawares a stealing tear / Witness'd how blissful was that hour."[10]

Moonlight romance was an established convention in visual culture as well. The American Pre-Raphaelite Thomas Charles Farrer's 1864 *Twilight* (fig. 8) is a gemlike oil in which two lovers embrace by the shore of a glassy lake, while over the hills beyond rises a sickle moon. Given the date, it is obvious that the tableau refers to the ongoing Civil War and the cruel fate that separated countless lovers for the duration—or, all too often, forever. In late 1864, Farrer gave the painting to the Artists' Fund Society for sale. Homer exhibited his *Skirmish in the Wilderness* (1864; New Britain Museum of American Art) at the same venue that year and surely must have seen Farrer's painting. Might it have lingered in his mind?[11]

Popular parlor music of the day was also rich in songs and images of lovers in the moonlight. Apprenticed to a lithographer in Boston, Homer was part of the music publishing business himself and even designed a handful of sheet-music covers. From early on, his mother played the piano (and no doubt sang), and the artist himself was musically literate.[12] Thus, it is safe to assume his familiarity with the romantic lunar iconography of popular music, as in "Ah! Would Our Eyes Had Never Met" of about 1845 (fig. 9), in which the moonlit ocean is the setting for two lovers gazing ardently into each other's eyes, the romantic mood enhanced by historical costume and a picturesque windmill. A later example (fig. 10) represents a modern couple affectionately entwined and leaning on a rail fence. Beyond, the full moon hovers low in the sky over a peaceful lake. Countless other songs paired love, the ocean, and moonlight. The cover of Stephen Foster's "Linger in Blissful Repose" (fig. 11) is literally oceanic, with the title words in an assortment of fancy fonts superimposed on the serene vista of sea and sky. As in Homer's watercolor, a bright full moon, its face partly veiled by wisps of clouds, casts a dazzling reflection on the water. The song, a romantic lullaby, bids the beloved to dream while melody flows around her.

Conceivably, Homer might have had any combination of precedents in mind when he set out to compose his own variation on the theme. But source hunting can take us only so far. There remains the question: why, just at that *particular* time, did Homer venture so far from his usual sunlit territory into the mysterious spaces of nocturnal romance?

As every Homer scholar knows, considerable speculation has surrounded the "mystery woman" whose alleged rejection of Homer's love so broke his heart that he remained a bachelor for the rest of his life.[13] Given the dearth of concrete evidence, there is no way to prove—or disprove—this supposition. Nonetheless, certain circumstances of the artist's life in the early 1870s allow us at least to muse on the traces of personal experience that the artist may have woven into *Moonlight.*

During his career as an illustrator for *Harper's Weekly* and other mass-marketed periodicals, Homer often drew scenes of modern courtship. Elizabeth Johns has carefully analyzed those scenes in light of Homer's own longing for romance as he struggled to achieve the financial stability necessary for him to marry. Johns also notes that the principal male figures in such scenes are often Homer look-alikes.[14] That alone, of course, hardly makes for a smoking gun.

But then there is Homer's friendship with the young artist Helena de Kay to consider. Although existing evidence is sketchy and circumstantial, there is enough to hint that she may have been the real mystery woman in his love life. The two traveled in the same New York artistic circles. In summer 1871 (and perhaps 1872), when both were in the Catskills—de Kay vacationing with her family and Homer in quest of picturesque subjects—their paths crossed as well. De Kay's friend Mary Hallock made note of this, writing effusively: "What an advantage to have Winslow Homer around! You'll pick up arey [ever] so many crumbs of wisdom."[15] On one of those occasions when Homer was "around," de Kay may have posed for him in the family's sunny summer garden. In *The Butterfly* (fig. 12), one of three oil sketches representing the same model, the young woman's

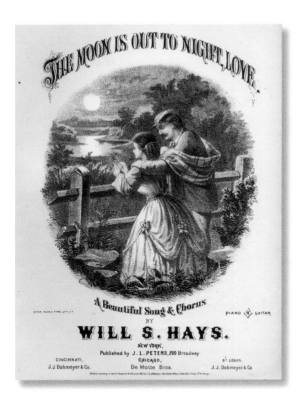

10. Will S. Hays, composer (1837–1907)
The Moon Is Out To Night, Love, 1867
Lithograph (sheet music cover); Snyder,
Black & Sturn, New York, lithographer;
J. L. Peters, New York, publisher.
Johns Hopkins University, Sheridan Libraries,
Lester S. Levy Sheet Music Collection

11. Stephen C. Foster, composer (1822–1864)
Linger in Blissful Repose, 1858
Lithograph (sheet music cover); Sarony, Major
& Knapp, New York, lithographer; Firth,
Pond & Co., New York, publisher. Johns Hopkins
University, Sheridan Libraries, Lester S. Levy
Sheet Music Collection

profile bears a striking resemblance to de Kay's, as evidenced by a contemporary photograph.[16]

The exact nature of the relationship between Homer and de Kay remains a puzzle. There is no doubt that he was attracted to the privileged and highly educated de Kay, who by all accounts was bright, winsome, and charming. One letter in particular hints at the warmth of Homer's feeling. In it, he enclosed some photographs of her. He considered them "failures" but vowed he would keep one for company nonetheless. However faint the resemblance, he told de Kay, "it's like a Beethoven symphony to me, as any remembrance of you will always be." For such a famously reserved and taciturn painter, these were florid words indeed. Homer signed the letter "believe me your most devoted, and true, and very sincere friend" and added a tiny sketch of a young woman—whose profile is much like Helena's—reaching for an out-size nosegay, inscribed: "This is a forget me not."[17]

Ultimately, de Kay married the poet and editor Richard Watson Gilder, whom she had met in 1872. Whether the tongue-tied painter ever had a chance against the refined and cultivated Gilder is an open question. Nor can we know if de Kay reciprocated Homer's feelings. That *he* had hopes, however, seems likely—hopes that would in the end be banished by de Kay's choice.[18]

Probably by no coincidence, Homer produced a string of courtship paintings during that time, starting with one in 1872 and culminating in a pictorial outburst of sorts in 1874. The earliest,

Waiting for an Answer (1872; Peabody Art Collection, Baltimore), represents a handsome young farmhand with a scythe, standing tensely at a distance from a comely young woman in pink, who avoids his earnest gaze as she ponders her decision. The 1874 *Girl in the Orchard* (Columbus Museum of Art, Ohio) shows the same young woman alone, her erstwhile suitor nowhere to be seen. Two others of 1874—*In the Garden* (collection of Mr. and Mrs. Paul Mellon) and *The Rustics* (private collection)—depict a young farmer wooing a housemaid who looks down at him from a window, as if to highlight the differences that keep them apart. The lost *Husking Corn* and *Course of True Love* ended the series, if such it was, both of them variations on the theme of misunderstanding, embarrassment, and rejection. It may be telling, too, that in 1874 Homer painted two oils, both titled *Enchanted* (Hood Museum of Art, Dartmouth College; and

private collection) and both roughly identical (albeit reversed) to the bottom half of *Flirting on the Sea-Shore and on the Meadow*. In all three, *two* rapt young country boys gaze at *one* little maiden. Might these scenes be veiled allusions to the rivalry between Homer and Gilder for Helena de Kay's affections?

Without *Moonlight*, though, none of this argument—speculative though it is—would hold water. Helena de Kay and Richard Watson Gilder were married on June 3, 1874. As a wedding gift, Homer presented de Kay with a somber portrait he had made of her (Museo Thyssen-Bornemisza, Madrid) perhaps as early as 1872 but now inscribed with the date of the ceremony that linked her life with another's. By that time, Homer had left New York for the summer, first heading to the Adirondacks and then repairing to East Hampton with Perry, there to paint *Moonlight*. Although summer travels

were the norm for artists, this year, perhaps, Homer may also have sought simply to escape.[19]

One crucial detail distinguishes the couple in *Moonlight* from Homer's other courtship tableaux: their social class. Although we cannot tell how they are dressed, the woman's open fan and her companion's walking stick signify urbanity, elegance, and leisure. Whereas all the rest are bumpkins and country lasses, these two are obviously middle class or higher. What we can glimpse of the man's finely tapered moustache closely resembles Homer's own, as seen, for example, in an 1869 photograph of the artist with his dog on the beach at Marshfield, Massachusetts (fig. 13). Here, as in many of his own paintings, the figure turns his back on us; all we can make out is the face in lost profile and just the tip of that telltale moustache.[20] The woman's open fan teasingly reminds us of *The Butterfly*, where the model in her filmy summer gown holds her fan fully open in the same way. Shorn of any rustic disguise, the couple on the beach might well be stand-ins for the artist and the woman now beyond his reach.

Helen Cooper has argued that *Moonlight* hints at Homer's "ambivalent relationship" with women. Slightly lower, the man positions himself as a supplicant, the handle of his cane along with the woman's open fan signaling "unmistakable sexual associations." The space between them vibrates with subtle tension. Her skirt brushes his knee; otherwise, the two sit apart, she looking away while he gazes up at her. Their "inner emotional landscape," Cooper maintains, "is echoed by their physical space," the "surreal" and dreamlike setting reinforcing their mood. Interestingly, contemporary critics responded to that mood as well. The *Brooklyn Eagle* was struck by the figures, so "boldly drawn against the moonlit water"; this, along with the breaking surf, gave "a weird effect to the scene."[21]

What Cooper so discerningly reads in the way Homer designed *Moonlight* pops into sharper focus if we factor in the story of Homer and de Kay. A suitor and lover if only in his dreams, Homer by 1874 had to face the fact that de Kay was lost to him for good. In *Moonlight*, the young woman has

turned away, refusing the attention of the man who leans so longingly toward her. The gap between them will never close, never even narrow. The site itself adds significance to the impasse between the two. Undoubtedly the setting is the ocean beach at East Hampton, which faces south by southeast. The moon rides high in the southern sky on its journey to the west. The ship on the horizon travels in the same direction, and even the breaking wave adds momentum to this trajectory away from the couple. They, however, are stationary. Their romance has run aground; quite literally, they are beached.

After 1874, courtship all but vanished from Homer's work. He returned to it for the last time in 1878, when he was an active member of the Tile Club, an artists' group that combined social evenings with the creation of decorative tiles. At one of their meetings, Homer recycled the top register of *Flirting on the Sea-Shore and on the Meadow* for his *Littoral Tile* (Detroit Institute of Arts). At another, he produced a blue-and-white tile (fig. 14) that seems to envision a happier ending for the melancholy *Moonlight*—if only in fantasy.

The scene is in tondo format, the corner spandrels of the enclosing square decorated with starfish against a grid of netting. On the breezy beach stands a young couple, arms lovingly entwined. They face out, toward the viewer, but they have eyes only for each other. The two are in antiquated costume, as if to set them at furthest remove from the present: this is happening not in real but in legendary time. Behind the man (who sports a Homeric moustache) a wave breaks, sending up a burst of foam; behind the woman the full moon shines, lighting the path of the schooner sailing off to the left. Her hair ribbons, flying in the breeze, provide a clue to meaning here. In the nineteenth century, such "flirtation ribbons," attached to hats or threaded through the hair, bore the name "suivez-moi, jeune homme" (follow me, young man).[22] The woman's body language

conveys that message as well: even as she looks back at her lover, she is already in movement, body swaying as she takes a step forward. Momentarily poised, the man leans toward her, ready to fall into line. Together, the two are about to embark on their journey through life. The deadlocked tension of *Moonlight* has given way to harmony and balance. Symbol of female divinity, the radiant moon is on her side. Suggestive of masculine energy, the effervescent wave is on his.[23]

Few paintings are transparently biographical. Even if they evolve from episodes in an artist's life, they do so in subtle and allusive ways. Yet given the clearly bracketed time span of Homer's courtship paintings and his own (possible) course of true but unrequited love, it is difficult to imagine *Moonlight* as merely the dispassionate representation of two anonymous figures on a beach at night. Aside from those few notes to Helena de Kay, Homer in his letters left no trace of his fantasies or desires. But in *Moonlight*, we catch a fleeting glimpse of his dreamy side, his shadow self as the romantic artist for whom night opened up a universe of wonder and mystery, and as a man who may have been mourning a dead romance. More eloquent than words could ever be, *Moonlight* opens a window into the artist's heart.

14. Winslow Homer (1836–1910)
Couple on the Shore, ca. 1878
Ceramic tile, 8 x 8 inches.
Collection of David and Laura Grey

NOTES

1. "Art Matters," *New York Evening Post*, October 31, 1874. Homer and Perry arrived in East Hampton some time in mid-July or a bit later. On July 25, the *New York Evening Post* in its "Art Notes" reported that the two were passing the summer there.

2. Van Wyck Brooks, *Opinions of Oliver Allston* (New York: Dutton, 1941), 54. John Butler Yeats (father of the poet) reported on Perry's reminiscences of that summer. According to Perry, he and Homer ate so many oysters that the shells gradually formed a pyramid, which finally toppled and "choked" the second room of the cabin.

3. "Calendar for Year 1874 (United States)," http://www.timeanddate.com/calendar/?year=1874&country=1.

4. Homer more often than not depicted fishermen with full beards, hence my assumption about the occupation of the man in *Flirting on the Sea-Shore and on the Meadow*.

5. Windmills were a familiar sight on Long Island. See Sr. Anne Frances Pulling and Gerald A. Leeds, *Windmills and Water Mills of Long Island* (Charleston: Arcadia, 1999).

6. Washington Allston, *Lectures on Art, and Poems*, ed. Richard Henry Dana Jr. (New York: Baker and Scribner, 1850), 103.

7. Henry T. Tuckerman, *Book of the Artists: American Artist Life* (New York: G. P. Putnam & Son, 1867), 150. On Homer's exposure to the Barbizon painters, see Erica E. Hirshler, "North Atlantic Drift: A Meditation on Winslow Homer and French Painting," in *Weatherbeaten: Winslow Homer and Maine*, ed. Thomas A. Denenberg (New Haven: Yale University Press, in association with the Portland Museum of Art, Maine, 2012), 71–83. Although it is tempting to believe that Homer in 1874 knew of James McNeill Whistler's poetic nocturnes, it is highly unlikely; see Marc Simpson, "Homer's Wine-Dark Seas," in *Winslow Homer: Poet of the Sea*, ed. Sophie Lévy (Giverny, France: Terra Foundation for American Art, 2006), 34–36. It is even more tempting to speculate that Homer somehow had knowledge of the uncannily similar moonlit landscapes by the early nineteenth-century German Romantic Caspar David Friedrich, but to date, no one has succeeded in establishing even the remotest possible connection.

8. Homer's copy was a gift from fellow Century Club member John Gourlie in 1872; see Patricia Junker, "Expressions of Art and Life in *The Artist's Studio in an Afternoon Fog*," in Philip C. Beam, *Winslow Homer in the 1890s: Prout's Neck Observed* (New York: Hudson Hills Press, in association with the Memorial Art Gallery, University of Rochester, 1990), 59.

9. George Chaplin Child, *The Great Architect: Benedicite; Illustrations of the Power, Wisdom, and Goodness of God, as Manifested in His Works* (New York: G. P. Putnam & Sons, 1871), 43–46. Elizabeth Johns has written that the scientific worldview endorsed by Child did not necessarily conflict with religious belief, natural theology being a long-established tenet of many Protestant traditions, including Homer's own; see Johns, *Winslow Homer: The Nature of Observation* (Berkeley: University of California Press, 2002), 138.

10. Edgar Allan Poe, "Annabel Lee [1849]," in *The Collected Works of Edgar Allan Poe*, ed. Thomas O. Mabbott, vol. 1, *Poems* (Cambridge, Mass.: Belknap Press of Harvard University Press, 1969), 477–79; William Lisle Bowles, "Discovery of Madeira," in *Poets and Poetry of England in the Nineteenth Century*, 3rd ed., ed. Rufus Wilmot Griswold (Philadelphia: Carey & Hart, 1846), 25.

11. On the Farrer and Homer submissions to the 1864 Artists' Fund Society sale, see Linda S. Ferber and William H. Gerdts, *The New Path: Ruskin and the American Pre-Raphaelites* (Brooklyn, New York: The Brooklyn Museum, 1985), 64; and Marc Simpson, *Winslow Homer: Paintings of the Civil War* (San Francisco: The Fine Arts Museums of San Francisco, 1988), 179.

12. Charles Savage Homer Sr. recalled in a letter that the "old piano" had been his first gift to his wife, Henrietta Benson Homer. Homer himself was conversant with music both popular and classical. In one letter he stated, "I think Die Meistersinger by Wagner is about as good as any Old Master"; in another he inscribed a few notes of music on a staff and added two stanzas of the song "Jimmy Crack Corn." Letters, Charles Savage Homer Sr. to his daughter-in-law Mrs. Charles (Mattie) Homer Jr., May 8, 1897; Winslow Homer to Mattie, May 1884; Winslow Homer letter fragment, Nov. 19, 1886, Winslow Homer and Homer Family Papers, Bowdoin College Museum of Art, Brunswick, Me.

13. See esp. Henry Adams, "The Identity of Winslow Homer's 'Mystery Woman,'" *Burlington Magazine* 132, no. 1045 (April 1990): 244–52.

14. Johns, *Winslow Homer*, chap. 2, esp. 55–72, 77–83.

15. Mary Hallock to Helena de Kay, undated, summer 1871 or 1872, no. 15, folio 14, box 6, Mary Hallock Foote Papers, Department of Special Collections, Stanford University Libraries, Stanford, Cal. My bracketed dates for this letter are based on the fact that the model in the 1872 oil sketches so strongly resembles de Kay, thus making it most likely the visit referred to by Hallock. However, there is also a possibility that Homer had been "around" de Kay the previous summer: "Art Notes," *New York Evening Post*, June 7, 1871, announced that Homer planned to spend the summer in the Catskills.

16. The photograph of de Kay is reproduced in *The Letters of Richard Watson Gilder* (Boston: Houghton Mifflin, 1916). The sketches are in the collection of the Cooper-Hewitt National Design Museum, New York. In all three, the model wears the same gauzy white summer dress; in two of them, she has what appears to be the same fan, open in one and folded shut in the other.

17. Winslow Homer, letter to Helena de Kay, June 19, [1872], Gilder Manuscripts, Lilly Library, Indiana University, Bloomington. It is not clear if Homer took photographs of de Kay herself or of her painted portrait, or if the photographer was someone else, but clearly, she was the subject represented. I assign the letter to 1872 because of the 51 West Tenth Street address Homer included under the June 19 date. This was the location of the Tenth Street Studio Building, where Homer had moved earlier that year.

18. For more on Homer and de Kay, see my article "The Courtship of Winslow Homer," *Magazine Antiques* 59 (February 2002): 68–75. In Lloyd Goodrich, edited and expanded by Abigail Booth Gerdts, *Record of Works by Winslow Homer*, vol. II (New York: Spanierman Gallery, 2005), 162–65, Gerdts disagrees with my interpretation of the Homer–de Kay romance but does not offer conclusive evidence to support this claim.

19. In "Art Notes," June 19, 1874, the *Daily Graphic* reported that Homer has just returned from a brief excursion to the Adirondacks, where he had obtained a number of "bold sketches" in watercolor. If he was in East Hampton by the latter half of July, then he presumably spent the time between trips in New York, but whatever the case, he was not in the city when the wedding took place.

20. Homer habitually depicted figures turning their backs to the viewer or with faces concealed by their headgear. The face of the man stooping down between two women in *Croquet Scene* (1866; The Art Institute of Chicago) is almost totally hidden by his round straw hat; the only identifiable feature is a moustache in Homer's style. Ted Loos, in "Casting Light on Homer's Dark Side," *Art & Antiques* 19, no. 3 (March 1996): 114, has argued persuasively that such figures are "much more alive for their universality" because we "have to work a little harder to peer past hat brims and around scarves to find a dialogue with them."

21. Helen A. Cooper, *Winslow Homer Watercolors* (New Haven: Yale University Press, in association with the National Gallery of Art, Washington, D.C., 1986), 44–47; *The Brooklyn Eagle*, March 8, 1875, quoted in Gordon Hendricks, *The Life and Work of Winslow Homer* (New York: Harry N. Abrams, 1979), 107. The title of the painting when it was displayed at the Brooklyn Watercolor Society show was *East Hampton Beach*. In 1875, Homer made a pencil sketch entitled *The Honeymoon* (private collection), said to represent his younger brother Arthur and his new wife, Alice Patch Homer. Here the man reclines, looking up at the woman, who, facing him, returns his gaze, in contrast to the alienated pair in *Moonlight*.

22. R. Turner Wilcox, *The Mode in Hats and Headdress*, rev. ed. (1959; repr., New York: Dover Publications, 2008), 232.

23. Some scholars have argued that Homer's splashing and foaming waves connote sexual excitement; see, for example, Jules Prown, "Winslow Homer in His Art," *Smithsonian Studies in American Art* 1, no. 1 (Spring 1987): 43.

THE EPISODIC WINSLOW HOMER

David Tatham

RETROSPECTIVE exhibitions of Winslow Homer's paintings have often left an impression that his career amounted to a long, gradual growth of his powers as an artist. This was, after all, the formative route followed by most other American painters of his generation as they absorbed influences from their teachers, from new art movements, and from each other. Homer's development as an artist differed. He had scarcely any academic training, paid little heed to art movements, and respected his fellow painters without following them.

Instead, his development came chiefly from a career-long sequence of self-motivated episodes of innovative new work. In these, he focused on a single subject with its permutations, on aspects of technique, on color and light—or, often, on all of these. Each episode differed in character from the others. Together they built, elaborated, and refined his style. Each episode produced at least a few works of significance within the Homer canon.

The Arkell Museum's Homer collection, which spans the entirety of the artist's career, offers insights into this episodic growth. Some episodes began and ended as if on schedule. Among these were Homer's intensive but quite different summers of painting in Gloucester (1873 and 1880), his year and a half in England (1881–82), and his forays into Florida and the Caribbean beginning in the mid-1880s. Other episodes began and became continuous or seasonally revived. His long association with the Adirondacks was one of these. Episodes sometimes ran concurrently or overlapped in time.

The earliest, longest, and most adventuresome overlap of Homer's episodes began with his decision to become a fine artist. In 1863, at age twenty-seven, he had established himself solidly as a well-paid freelance illustrator in black and white. His work appeared often in the nation's leading pictorial magazine, *Harper's Weekly*.

15. Peter A. Juley & Son, photographers
Winslow Homer, Prout's Neck, Maine
Peter A. Juley & Son Collection,
Smithsonian American Art Museum, J0001697

When early in 1863 he began to exhibit oil paintings, he became a "real" artist in the eyes of other painters. In this first episode of painting, he soon depicted Civil War subjects differently than he had as an illustrator, and this began his remarkable rise in the American art world.

His move from illustrator to painter had carried with it two major implications. First, as a painter he would address a much smaller but more sophisticated audience than he had as an illustrator, and the audience would include art critics.

He would now need to contend with published assessments of his work. The second implication of his shift was that his income as a painter would be at the mercy of the art market. *Harper's Weekly* had paid him cash on the barrelhead as soon as it accepted an illustration. In contrast, the time and effort he put into a painting would bring him nothing until the painting sold, if indeed it ever did. Because his paintings sold slowly, he augmented what little income they produced by continuing to draw for the Harper's firm and other publishers. He did so for an additional dozen years.

Despite the disappointing sales of his early oils, he had nonetheless begun well, for his Civil War paintings attracted a respectful audience of newspaper and magazine critics. This established him as an artist of promise. In 1866, nearly a year after the war, he fulfilled that promise with his *Prisoners from the Front* (fig. 16). This painting depicts a Union officer on a recently bombarded but now quiet battleground. He calmly questions three guarded Confederate prisoners of different ages, social classes, and attitudes. To many Northerners, the painting concerned not only the conclusion of a devastating conflict but also a historic disparity between two cultures, North and South, their pasts and prospects.

Critics and others acclaimed the painting for the originality and complexity of its concept. It sold immediately and soon traveled on loan to Paris to become part of the American painting section of the 1867 Exposition Universelle. With this, Homer brought his first episode as a fine

16. Winslow Homer (1836–1910)
Prisoners from the Front, 1866
Oil on canvas, 24 x 38 inches.
The Metropolitan Museum of Art, New York, N.Y.,
Gift of Mrs. Frank B. Porter, 1922 (22.207)

artist to a close. Critics and others had supposed that he would exploit the success of *Prisoners* by creating other works of its kind, perhaps on further nationally meaningful subjects such as Western Expansion or Reconstruction. But he did not.

Prisoners became the end of his beginnings. He had learned from it that a period of intense work toward a single goal—one that embraced many variations along the way—enabled him to refine his concepts, solve problems of technique, and make his subject wholly his own. Having completed that episode, he would then move on to a new, more challenging or adventuresome episode with his skills now enhanced by what he had learned from its predecessor.

As Homer embarked on new episodes after the war, some critics expressed regret that he no longer produced paintings that in subject and manner echoed *Prisoners*. Homer viewed the matter differently. He summed up his view of *Prisoners* a few years after its great success with his remark, "I'm sick of hearing about that picture."[1]

His first post–Civil War episodes had depicted subjects from ordinary, often rural, American life. This move from a subject of historic importance to those of everyday experience cost him the support of many critics. He painted croquet matches, women and children at leisure on sunny (or cloudy) beaches, fellow painters at work on New England heights, rustic lads in meadows and schoolhouses, farmers pausing from labors in their fields, and other transitory moments of ordinary life. None of these subjects had the intellectual underpinnings or the quiet drama of his great painting of the war. Critics found these subjects unworthy of the best of Civil War artists.

Yet in all these works he demonstrated an independence of thought that distinguished him from his fellow American artists. Like many of them he painted American life, though he differed in the subjects he selected, his treatment of them, and the often inelegant but effective directness of his style. That he was largely self-taught, rather than a product of academy or apprentice training, probably had much to do with the distinctiveness of his work.

17. Winslow Homer (1836–1910)
Beach Scene, ca. 1869
Oil on canvas, 11 ½ x 9 ⅖ inches.
Museo Thyssen-Bornemisza,
Madrid, Spain, Inv.Nr: CTB 1985.12

But to anyone who looked beyond the subjects—and few critics seem to have spent much time doing so—these oil paintings demonstrated Homer's rapidly growing if idiosyncratic development of technique. His brushwork became freer, his surfaces more tactile. He used color and light in more varied and vital ways. The logic of his compositions now followed his instincts as well as academic tradition, and with good effect.

Even as he reformed his painterly manner in his oils of the late 1860s and early 1870s, critics took him to task for departing from the rules of "good" painting. They reserved praise chiefly for new paintings by other artists that in subject and style adhered closely to what the era's academies of fine art prescribed as tradition-tested

18. Winslow Homer (1836–1910)
On the Beach, ca. 1869
Oil on canvas, 15 x 24 ½ inches.
Arkell Museum at Canajoharie,
Gift of Bartlett Arkell, 1932. Cat. no. 2

ways of making art. This was hardly possible in the case of a talent so strongly individualistic as Homer's. To read some of the critics' reviews is to confirm Lloyd Goodrich's observation in his 1944 biography of Homer that "American criticism has seldom been at as low a level as in the decade after the Civil War—either incredibly naïve or pseudo-sophisticated in a way that was even worse."[2]

A rare recorded instance of Homer's response to offensive criticism survives in the case of his oil painting *On the Beach* (ca. 1869; fig. 18). It was originally part of a much larger work, *Low Tide*, but in 1870, Homer withdrew the canvas from the run of the winter exhibition at the National Academy of Design—an astonishing act in itself. In his studio, he cut two sections from the canvas (one of them became *On the Beach*) and destroyed or obliterated the rest. The lost parts included parts of the sky and the beach as well as a sandy foreground with children's shoes.[3]

One of the offending critics had asked rhetorically about *Low Tide*: "How an artist of acknowledged worth in a certain field of art, could permit this horror to leave his studio is simply incomprehensible to us."[4] (His distancing description of Homer as an artist of "acknowledged worth in a certain field" very likely refers to other critics' positive reviews of his Civil War paintings.) This reviewer then proceeded to describe *Low Tide's* details in terms certain to be distressing to any except the most hard-shelled of painters.

Scarcely any critic seemed to accept that in the three years that separated *Prisoners* from *Low Tide*, Homer had become a painter with a new vision. He now depicted fleeting moments of ordinary, mostly quiet events and nothing weightier. Moreover, in painterly technique he had moved ahead steadily, too steadily for many of his critics to comprehend. The heavy impasto on the closest wave in *On the Beach* was, for instance, a fresh addition to his repertoire, and one little-used by most American artists. The same critic of *Low Tide* described this impasto as produced by Homer's "throwing his dirty sponge . . . at the canvas."[5]

The liveliness of the girls who get their feet wet on the beach introduced figures in motion with a vitality unseen in Homer's earlier paintings. The reflections in wet sand intensify a sense of fleeting time, and this, too, represented a new development in his work. The waves count as among the earliest instances of his naturalistic painting of the sea in motion. On the horizon are specks of white, dismissed by some critics but easily identified by the sharp-eyed as sails. In 1870, all these things in Homer's work struck critics as uncomfortably new and unwelcome.

Though Homer had been to Paris for ten months in 1866–67, little in *On the Beach* suggests any French influence, except perhaps an analytic sharpening of his already strong powers of observation. The other surviving section of *Low Tide*, titled *Beach Scene* (ca. 1869; fig. 17), depicts more sand and water and a group of younger, livelier children at play in the waves. Its animated figures act as a foil to the quieter propriety of those in *On the Beach.*

Much of Homer's new work continued to bother and even confuse some critics throughout the next decade. They found fault not only in his steady advances in technique but also in the notable variety of his subjects. What he chose to paint one year often had nothing to do with what he would paint the next, and this, of course, was a function of his episodic approach. Because his work of the 1870s was neither formulaic nor predictable, critics found it difficult to categorize or classify him, or to identify the organic growth within his work. These were things that critics very much wanted to be able to do.

Homer further complicated matters for his reviewers when in 1873 he adopted a second medium: painting in watercolors. This became a major

episode in his development—or, more accurately, a long series of episodes. By the end of the 1870s, critics had begun to agree that Homer counted as the greatest American master of the medium. Over the next quarter century, following his watercolor campaigns in many sites, his stature rose ever higher.

Of course, not all reviews of his 1870s oils were wearisome or even offensive. *The Country School* (1871; Saint Louis Art Museum), for instance, received much praise. But in a decade of recurrent negative reviews, a rare burst of near-unanimous praise was not enough to alter one's problematic reputation. Still, in time a general reluctance to praise Homer's work began to change. Consider one reviewer, Mariana van Rensselaer, a critic of strongly held views, who as late as 1879 had expressed dislike for a group of Homer's Houghton Farm watercolors. Here is a brief excerpt from her review:

> *Mr. Winslow Homer exhibited no less than twenty-nine numbers, in which the various yet cognate eccentricities of his brush were fully represented. . . . He turns in preference to most unbeautiful figures of wooden outline and glaring diversity of tint. . . . Mr. Homer must have some idea of the indistinct crudeness of his own work both in outline and in color.*[6]

Then, in 1883, when she had become highly enthusiastic about his British work of the early 1880s, she looked back at his earlier years to recall her former marked dislike for his work. "As a youthful visitor to our exhibitions . . . I remember to have hated Mr. Homer in quite vehement and peculiar fashion." But she then added, and other critics must have nodded in agreement, that her dislike of Homer's earlier paintings acknowledged his "individuality and his force, and also his freedom from the neat little waxy prettinesses of idea and expression which are so alien to true art."[7]

By the mid-1880s, the worst of the critical reviews had passed, though Homer remained touchy for the rest of his career about what he

(Detail) Winslow Homer, **Contraband**, 1875 (see cat. 9)

The title of this image refers to the bedraggled African American boy. It establishes him as a person born into slavery but freed by Union troops to become property of the federal government for the duration of the war. The adult figure's Zouave military uniform summons up memories of a war that had ended ten years earlier. The theatricality of the image, including its setting, is unique within this episode and rare within Homer's life's work.

Nothing in the image suggests a source in Homer's body of Civil War paintings, drawings, and illustrations. He seems certain to have devised the entire work in 1875. That the painting is a product of the mid-1870s rather than the war years is confirmed by its watercolor medium—Homer had begun to use it for painting only in 1873. Further, the model for the boy had posed for Homer in several other works of 1874–75. Nothing has yet been found to suggest that *Contraband* illustrates a text of its time or depicts a scene from a once popular stage work. A more likely account of the image is that it is an allegorical comment on one of the major issues of its day: the imminent collapse of the federal Reconstruction programs. This approach to a subject was most unusual for Homer, but the subject itself was highly unusual.

In such a reading the tired Zouave personifies the federal government's fading support for its Reconstruction programs, including the Freedmen's Bureau schools. These had been established by the Lincoln administration to bring former slaves into the world of literacy. The beseeching boy personifies the plea of a younger generation of African Americans to preserve the program.[9] Such an interpretation helps to explain Homer's sharply focused and meticulously executed attention on two figures who offer comparatively few conventional rewards of the sort expected from Homer and who appear in no "real" setting.

By 1873, when withdrawal of federal troops from the South meant that some former Confederate states offered no federal protection to oppressed African Americans or to white or black Freedmen's Bureau workers, little was left of the earlier spirit of uplift. By 1876, Reconstruction was as good as

perceived as unwarranted slights of his work. This and other aspects of his "curmudgeonly" late-life manner, especially toward persons in the art world, may someday be traced to his need over the years to suffer, mostly in silence, earlier negative reviews. By the mid-1880s, when he had moved to the coast of Maine, he sent new work not only to New York but also to dealers and exhibitions in Boston, where critics were friendlier.

But even back in the 1870s, Homer on rare occasions produced a work of unusual visual interest that differed so much from others in its episode that critics (and later Homer commentators) found little if anything to say about it. One such work is the Arkell's 1875 watercolor *Contraband*, a small and atypical work from Homer's major episode concerning African American life a decade after the Civil War.[8]

dead. This historical moment was summed up in the 1930s by W. E. B. Du Bois, in his succinct observation of the circumstances of American black life in these years: "The slave went free; stood a brief moment in the sun; then moved back again toward slavery."[10]

Homer, like any educated American of his time, knew a good deal about Reconstruction. He learned enough about its Freedmen's Schools in his mid-1870s visits to Virginia to allude to their success in another of his works from this episode, the oil painting *Sunday Morning in Virginia* (1877; Cincinnati Art Museum).[11] Here an older, now literate, African American girl reads aloud from a bible to younger children. Because the South had prohibited the teaching of reading to generations of slaves, this young reader has almost certainly become literate at a Freedmen's School. Homer intimates in his painting that as she reads aloud, she also teaches reading to the children.

Works from Homer's African American episode of the mid-1870s brought him some praise from critics but little acclaim.[12] The figures, their settings, and their relationships came from a world quite foreign to most reviewers. Clarence Cook, one of New York's more astute critics, who regularly praised Homer's innate gifts while just as regularly finding fault with the uses to which he put them, reflected this uneasiness when he described the model for the boy in *Contraband* (from his presence in another of Homer's paintings) as a "monkeyish little darky-boy."[13]

During this episode's long span, Homer engaged himself in briefer overlapping episodes. In oils he painted several finely detailed full-lengths of handsomely dressed young women, sometimes posed in decorative garden settings. He also produced several striking watercolors of young women in interiors, less elegantly attired. But the painting that received almost universal praise at this point, even from Cook, was Homer's oil *Breezing Up*, also known as *A Fair Wind* (1876; National Gallery of Art, Washington, D.C.).

Homer had developed this work in phases from watercolors he had painted in his Gloucester episode of 1873. Several critics described it as Homer's "best" painting since *Prisoners*. But, as had happened with *The Country School*, after years of recurrent negative or slighting reviews, a chorus of unanimous praise scarcely altered its maker's reputation as a "problem" painter.

At some point, perhaps in the 1880s, Cook wrote a brief summary of Homer and his career. He did so for a volume of artist biographies published in 1888, saying, "No picture has been painted in America in our day that made so deep an appeal to the feelings of the people as his *Prisoners to the Front*." Cook then continued on in ways largely repetitive of what he had expressed about that painting over the years.[14] He then added that after some years Homer "had disappeared for a time, living in the country, fishing and hunting, and painting very little, or at any rate showing few pictures."

In saying this, Cook all but admitted that he had not kept up with Homer's career. Nothing in his statement of Homer's post-*Prisoners* career is accurate. If by "disappeared" he meant merely that Homer had moved out of Manhattan, then his choice of words was both odd and misleading, for Homer appeared at New York exhibitions periodically even after he had moved to Prout's Neck on the coast of Maine. Cook erred in suggesting that Homer painted or exhibited little after the 1870s. The 1880s brought forth a sequence of major oils concerning humankind and the sea, as well as many dozens of striking paintings in watercolor.

When Homer reached the final decades of his career as a painter, it would have been clear that the two concerns of his beginnings as a painter—income and criticism—had come to very different conclusions. After a slow start, the income he earned from his paintings gradually picked up. By the 1880s it had become substantial. In his last decade he had reason to consider himself comfortably well-to-do, if not modestly wealthy (at least by the standards of the State of Maine). But his long encounter with critics' assessments had been, until his last years, a bitter experience. While his paintings still astonish us, his critics' commentaries on them are, by our standards, unseeing, amateurish, misguided, or worse.

To read his critics is to be reminded of how fortunate the American art world of the mid-twentieth century was to have as its leading critics Clement Greenberg and Harold Rosenberg (always contending), Leo Steinberg (when he took off his Renaissance historian's cap and turned his attention to Jasper Johns), and a host of others. These critics, each in a different way, found the high art of its time to be both a reflection of the deepest currents of American society and a product of each maker's complex of intellectual and emotional drives. As the Arkell's collection makes clear, Homer survived the inadequacy of his generation's critics and achieved things that would find respect in Greenberg's generation.

NOTES

1. Quoted in Lloyd Goodrich, *Winslow Homer* (New York: Macmillan, in association with the Whitney Museum of American Art, 1944), 51.

2. Goodrich, *Winslow Homer*, 50.

3. Some indication of *Low Tide's* painted imagery may be found in Homer's wood-engraved illustration of the same title published in *Every Saturday*, August 6, 1870, and reproduced in fig. 19, cat. entry 2. See also David Tatham, *Winslow Homer and the Pictorial Press* (Syracuse: Syracuse University Press, 2003), 172.

4. "Fine Arts: The Winter Exhibition of the National Academy of Design," *New York Evening Mail*, November 6, 1869, quoted in Margaret C. Conrads, *Winslow Homer and the Critics: Forging a National Art in the 1870s* (Princeton, N.J.: Princeton University Press, in association with the Nelson-Atkins Museum of Art, Kansas City, 2001), 20. Conrads offers an illuminating survey and a thorough analysis of published reviews of Homer's works from the late 1860s through the 1870s.

5. "Fine Arts," quoted in Conrads, *Winslow Homer and the Critics.*

6. Mariana Griswold van Rensselaer, "Recent Pictures in New York," *American Architect and Building News* 5 (March 22, 1879): 93–94, quoted in Conrads, *Winslow Homer and the Critics*, 155–56.

7. Mrs. Schuyler (Mariana) van Rensselaer, "An American Artist in England," *Century* 27 (November 1883): 15.

8. In perhaps the only contemporary notice of the painting's imagery, a reviewer for *The Nation* wrote that "a Zouave, armed with the fragrant canteen, is making friends with a little contraband, the soldier, relieved against black, is modelled with the skill of [Jehan Georges] Vibert or [Édouard] Detaille; but the completion of this single figure seems a caprice or an accident." "Fine Arts: Ninth Exhibition of the Water-Color Society," *Nation* 22 (February 17, 1876): 120, quoted in Lloyd Goodrich, edited and expanded by Abigail Booth Gerdts, *Record of Works by Winslow Homer*, vol. II (New York: Spanierman Gallery, 2005), 382. If by "fragrant canteen" the critic implies that the soldier is sharing an alcoholic drink with the boy, the reading is highly unlikely for a work exhibited at the American Watercolor Society, or for any work by Homer whose propriety in all things was one of his

hallmarks. By placing Homer in the shadow of two French artists—Detaille was widely admired for his paintings of figures in military dress—the critic minimized attention to Homer while promoting his own claims as a connoisseur.

9. A few traditional allegorical elements grace the top of Homer's wood-engraved illustration *Seeing the Old Year Out*, published in *Harper's Weekly* 5 (January 5, 1861). More subtle and original allusions appear in many of his paintings. For a thoroughgoing consideration of such informal allegory in Homer's oil *Weaning the Calf* (1875; North Carolina Museum of Art), with much useful close reading and argumentation, see Kenneth Haltman, "Antipastoralism in Early Winslow Homer," *Art Bulletin* 80, no. 1 (March 1998): 93–112.

10. W. E. B. Du Bois, *Black Reconstruction: An Essay Toward the History of the Part Which Black Folk Played in the Attempt to Reconstruct Democracy in America* (New York: Harcourt, Brace, 1935), 30.

11. For a useful introduction to these paintings and other of Homer's African American subjects, see Peter H. Wood and Karen C. C. Dalton, *Winslow Homer's Images of Blacks: The Civil War and Reconstruction Years* (Austin: University of Texas Press, 1988).

12. A critic from the *New York Evening Post* observed as part of a longer review that "Mr. Homer has treated these simple themes with fidelity and freshness. His negroes are real negroes, children of the southern soil. . . . The figures possess remarkable roundness and relief, and the facial expressions are distinct studies for the spectator. In subject, conception and execution these works are most refreshingly original." See "Pictures for the Paris Exhibition," *New York Evening Post*, January 26, 1878, quoted in Conrads, *Winslow Homer and the Critics*, 127. While this was hardly discerning criticism, it at least avoided the quibbles, disappointing judgments, and dismissive rhetoric that peppered the reviews of many of Homer's works in these years.

13. "The Water-Color Exhibition," *New York Daily Tribune*, February 19, 1876, quoted in Conrads, *Winslow Homer and the Critics*, 91. Cook refers in this way to the model as Homer depicted him in *Taking Sunflower to Teacher* (1875, Georgia Museum of Art, Athens). The teacher of the title may have taught at a Freedmen's School. The boy model appears in several of Homer's works in 1875.

14. Clarence Cook, *Art and Artists of Our Time* (New York: Selmar Hess, 1888; repr., New York: Garland, 1978), 256–58.

Arkell Catalogue of Winslow Homer Works

THIS CATALOGUE represents the twenty works by Winslow Homer that Bartlett Arkell gave to the Canajoharie Library and Art Gallery (now called the Arkell Museum at Canajoharie), along with the four works that he retained in his personal collection. The works are listed in chronological order, with those undatable at the end. Dimensions are given in inches, with height before width. All inscriptions appearing on the face of the work are listed as they appear, while only significant inscriptions on the reverse side (verso) are listed. The abbreviations *LL* and *LR* refer to the location of the inscriptions as either "lower left" or "lower right."

Arkell Museum curatorial files contain correspondence that assisted with the history of ownership (provenance) of each work. Macbeth Gallery records, Archives of American Art, Smithsonian Institution played an important part in our understanding of the Homer collection's history.

This catalogue would not be complete, or as accurate, without the years of research begun by Lloyd Goodrich, edited and expanded by Abigail Booth Gerdts, and published as *Record of Works by Winslow Homer*, vols. I–III (New York: Spanierman Gallery, 2005–8); vol. IV (New York: Goodrich-Homer Art Education Project, 2012). The definitive authority on Homer's art, *Record of Works* currently includes all of the artist's known works through 1889. The fifth and final volume will be published in 2014. The format and early history of the provenance section of *Record of Works* have been adhered to in the Arkell catalogue. Each entry includes the Arkell Museum object number, followed by the number assigned to it in the Goodrich and Gerdts (GG) *Record of Works*. This multivolume publication is also referred to as *GG Record* in the endnotes.

The following catalogue entries were written by Diane E. Forsberg (DEF) and Martha Hoppin (MH).

(Detail) Winslow Homer, **Woman on the Beach, Marshfield**, 1874 (see cat. 5)

1   IN FRONT OF THE GUARD-HOUSE (Punishment for Intoxication) 1863

Oil on canvas, 17 x 13 inches
Inscribed LL: Homer 1863
Arkell Museum at Canajoharie, Gift of Bartlett Arkell, 1941
317108 (GG 201)

Provenance: Charles S. Homer Jr., n.d.; Mrs. Charles S. Homer Jr., by bequest, 1917; (William Macbeth, Inc., ca. 1937); Bartlett Arkell, 1941

IN FRONT OF THE GUARD-HOUSE depicts a form of Union army discipline Homer presumably witnessed at the time of the Civil War. An errant soldier has been forced to carry a heavy log while perched atop a box, which greatly restricts his range of movement. His downward glance and shift in stance show that he is tired. A guard patrols with a bayoneted rifle that is exaggeratedly slim and pointed in contrast to the log. Both men stand in the immediate foreground, next to a large barrel that provides compositional balance and a slightly enigmatic note. Perhaps the barrel alludes to liquor and thus led to the change in title; Bartlett Arkell acquired the work as *Punishment for Intoxication*. Recent scholarship has suggested that while intoxication was typically punished by having the offender walk around in a large barrel or remain in solitary confinement, several types of rule-breaking earned the punishment Homer pictured.[1]

When the Civil War broke out in April 1861, Homer had been living in New York City for almost two years. He had moved there from Boston in 1859 and soon found work as a freelance illustrator. In the fall of 1861, *Harper's Weekly*—the country's leading illustrated journal—sent him to record the Union army encamped near Washington. The next spring, he joined the troops at Yorktown, Virginia.[2] His mother reported that he remained at Yorktown for about two months, "suffered much," and "was without food 3 days at a time."[3] In between visits to the front, he returned to his life in New York City and began to paint in oils. His on-the-spot drawings of the war were published as wood engravings in *Harper's Weekly* and served as the basis for his paintings. *In Front of the Guard-House*, which most likely stemmed from Homer's experiences in Yorktown, was among the earliest of these. Like almost all of his Civil War canvases, it captures life in camp rather than in battle. In 1864, Homer sent it to the National Academy of Design's annual exhibition, and he reused the painting's theme as one in a series of lithographs, *Life in Camp*, published by Louis Prang in 1864.[4]   MH

NOTES

1. Marc Simpson, *Winslow Homer: Paintings of the Civil War* (San Francisco: Fine Arts Museums of San Francisco, 1988), 161–63.

2. Sally Mills, "A Chronology of Homer's Early Career, 1859–1866," in Simpson, *Winslow Homer*, 20–21, and GG, Record I, 120, 123, note that he made this trip on his own, not for *Harper's Weekly*, and that he observed the army in Virginia once more in 1864.

3. Quoted in Gordon Hendricks, *The Life and Work of Winslow Homer* (New York: Harry N. Abrams, 1979), 50, where it is cited as "letter in a private collection."

4. GG, Record I, 240, evaluates the Homer family legend that it was Charles Homer Jr.'s purchase of *In Front of the Guard-House* that encouraged the artist to continue painting. The Prang version of the composition includes a second soldier carrying a log.

2 ON THE BEACH ca. 1869

Oil on canvas, 15 x 24 ½ inches
Inscribed LR: HOMER
Arkell Museum at Canajoharie, Gift of Bartlett Arkell, 1932
317105 (GG 360)

Provenance: Charles S. Homer Jr., by bequest, 1910; Mrs. Charles S. Homer Jr., by bequest, 1917; Arthur P. Homer, by bequest; (William Macbeth, Inc., 1932); Bartlett Arkell, 1932

WINSLOW HOMER cut this painting from a much larger work, *Low Tide*, which depicted activity on the beach at Long Branch, New Jersey. *Low Tide* was harshly criticized when it was exhibited at the National Academy of Design's winter exhibition in 1869. Critics were not impressed by the ambitious work—with its arrangement of broad bands of sky, sea, and beach, and numerous groups of people—calling it "a Watering-place deformity" and referring to sections of the work as an "unhappy accident on canvas."[1]

It is not known exactly when Homer destroyed the original *Low Tide*, but it was most likely a reaction to the critics' biting comments. Homer cut out at least two sections of the canvas. The other known section is a vertical painting of children playing in the waves, *Beach Scene* (fig. 17; Museo Thyssen-Bornemisza, Madrid). One of the critics of *Low Tide* noted that individual groups of people

in the painting were "charmingly posed little pictures in themselves—it would not be the work of Homer if it had not a lurking charm somewhere."[2] Homer was well known for his charming magazine illustrations, and he did use the "little pictures" from the large painting for a wood engraving called *Low Tide*, which was published in *Every Saturday* in 1870 (fig. 19). The five young women wading in the water on the left side of *On the Beach* appear in reverse in the engraving. The engraving is more densely peopled than is *On the Beach* and includes several groups of figures, some of which appear in *Beach Scene*, along with additional foreground figures that may have never been in the larger painting. When Homer selected the section of the canvas that is known as *On the Beach*, he was using different criteria than he used to choose images for magazine illustrations. The *Harper's* illustration focuses on activities that encourage a narrative interpretation, whereas the painting retains his aesthetic concern for color and composition.

Two-thirds of *On the Beach* remains a horizontal seascape without figures. Homer's larger work, *Low Tide*, had been assailed for its "three grand horizontal layers" of sky, sea, and beach, which the *New York Evening Mail* critic said looked "like rock strata." A writer for the *Express* remained more open to the seascape's "force and originality" and, though he did not consider the painting very good, thought that in its "total disregard of all conventionality, lies the secret of its success."[3]

19. Winslow Homer (1836–1910)
Low Tide
Every Saturday, August 6, 1870.
Wood engraving, 11 x 15 inches.
Arkell Museum at Canajoharie, Museum Purchase

Bartlett Arkell had no idea that his painting was once part of a larger, controversial canvas when he purchased the work in 1932. He called *On the Beach* "soul inspiring."[4] No one today would see the work as shocking in either subject matter or composition, and many would agree with Arkell, who wrote in 1944 that "this picture. . . has done more to exalt my spirit and put me in another world."[5] DEF

NOTES

1. "National Academy of Design. Winter Exhibition," *New York Tribune*, December 4, 1869; and "Fine Arts: The Winter Exhibition of the National Academy of Design," *New York Evening Mail*, November 6, 1869, quoted in Nicolai Cikovsky Jr., "Modern and National," in Nicolai Cikovsky Jr. and Franklin Kelly, *Winslow Homer* (Washington, D.C.: National Gallery of Art, 1995), 81. See Cikovsky, 81–84, for a complete discussion of the original painting, its critics, and the smaller paintings (now in Canajoharie and Madrid) that were cut from the original. The exact size of the original painting is not known, but the *New York Evening Mail* critic believed it to be "twelve square feet of canvas at the least."

2. "Fine Arts," quoted in Cikovsky, *Winslow Homer*, 83.

3. Margaret C. Conrads, *Winslow Homer and the Critics: Forging a National Art in the 1870s* (Princeton, N.J.: Princeton University Press in association with The Nelson-Atkins Museum of Art, Kansas City, 2001), 20–22. Conrads explains that it was Homer's "lack of conventionality in compositional structure" that made critics at the *New York Evening Post*, November 24, 1969, and the *Express*, November 24, 1869, see certain aspects of *Low Tide* as successful.

4. Letter from Bartlett Arkell to Lloyd Goodrich, Whitney Museum of American Art, July 18, 1944, copy in Arkell Museum curatorial files.

5. Letter from Bartlett Arkell to Lloyd Goodrich, July 18, 1944.

3 THE SEE-SAW ca. 1873

Watercolor over graphite on wove paper, 7 1/4 x 13 1/2 inches
Arkell Museum at Canajoharie, Gift of Bartlett Arkell, 1932
31798 (GG 455)

Provenance: Charles S. Homer Jr., by bequest, 1910; Arthur B. Homer, by gift, 1910; Charles L. Homer, by bequest, 1916; (William Macbeth, Inc., 1931); Bartlett Arkell, 1931, for the Canajoharie Library and Art Gallery

HOMER FIRST TOOK UP WATERCOLOR as a serious pursuit during the two months he spent in Gloucester, Massachusetts, in the summer of 1873. Like the other watercolors he painted then, *The See-Saw* features children at play. A popular subject after the Civil War, children came to symbolize both nostalgic yearning for an innocent past and optimistic hope for the future. Along with his colleagues in the field of genre painting, among them Eastman Johnson and John George Brown, Homer depicted boys and girls in idyllic rural settings throughout the decade. One of his best-known oil paintings, the scene of country children titled *Snap the Whip* (Butler Institute of American Art, Youngstown), preceded the Gloucester works by only one year.

The See-Saw typifies Homer's Gloucester watercolors in representing young boys by the sea. In other examples, they sit on rocks, build toy boats, watch the water, or row dories. The boys in *The See-Saw* have devised a makeshift game in which the center boy balances the two ends of a wooden plank. The composition itself wittily reinforces the notion of balance. Two boys sit on either end of the seesaw, and repeating triangular forms—the rock under the plank, the central boy's figure, and the roofs beyond—create the space.

Two sailboats on the left match the two boys on the right. The arrangement of sunlit figures against a background of rocks or sea is also characteristic of Homer's scenes from this summer. Some Gloucester compositions are more simplified than this one, which includes buildings and even the word "bait" clearly visible on one of the sheds. On the other hand, Homer quickly drew and then dashed color on the children on the left, leaving their forms roughly defined.

By the time of his Gloucester visit, Homer had established himself as a painter in oils, but he earned his living as an illustrator. The wood engraving *See-Saw—Gloucester, Massachusetts*, published in *Harper's Weekly* the following year, combines the boys and the setting from *The See-Saw* with another Gloucester watercolor, *Girls with Lobster* (Cleveland Museum of Art).[1] The summer of 1873 served another important purpose. Homer may have initially turned to watercolor because it offered a way to sketch in color, but he soon discovered that he was good at it. The medium was also growing in popularity with artists and collectors. Finding he could sell his watercolors, Homer gave up illustration in 1875. Today he is recognized as America's greatest watercolor master. MH

NOTES

1. See D. Scott Atkinson and Jochen Wierich, *Winslow Homer in Gloucester* (Chicago: Terra Museum of American Art, 1990), 19–20, 80, for discussion and illustration of the wood engraving, which was published in the September 12, 1874, issue of *Harper's*.

4 BOY ON ROCKS ca. 1873

Watercolor over graphite on wove paper, 8⅜ x 13½ inches
Inscribed LR: Homer 187[?]
Arkell Museum at Canajoharie, Gift of Bartlett Arkell, 1932
317100 (GG 451)

Provenance: Charles S. Homer Jr., by bequest, 1910; Arthur B. Homer, by gift, 1910; Charles L. Homer, by bequest, 1916; (William Macbeth, Inc., 1931); Bartlett Arkell, 1931, for the Canajoharie Library and Art Gallery

HOMER SPENT the summer of 1873 in Gloucester, Massachusetts. The watercolors he painted there, which include *Boy on Rocks*[1] and *The See-Saw* (see entry 3), represent his first efforts to take advantage of the medium's special properties. In *Boy on Rocks*, a young child nestles into an expanse of brown that takes up over three-quarters of the picture. No other watercolor from this summer put so much emphasis on rocks. The boy's white shirt and hat catch the light, but his figure blends into his setting. Homer's major interest was in capturing the shapes and surfaces of this large outcropping. The massive shaded area presented a challenge, which he met by varying his brushwork over a broad, brown wash and adding darker brown tones. He used opaque white touches for highlights on the boy's hat and for the ocean spray on the rocks.

The boy looks out to sea, a common image in Homer's work from this summer. Although Homer depicted sunny days and children at play, it is possible to imagine a darker side to his scenes of boys on the waterfront, especially in one like *Boy on Rocks*, with its overall brown tone and lone figure. Given the routine loss of life suffered by Gloucester's fishing fleets, the activity of watching the horizon could convey an underlying wariness as well as the freedom of a lazy summer day. In one watercolor from 1873, *Waiting for Dad* (Mills College Art Museum, Oakland, Cal.), Homer made the connection explicit.[2] MH

NOTES

1. The last digit of the date is not visible. When Bartlett Arkell acquired this work from William Macbeth's gallery, Macbeth wrote that he should title it *Boy on Rocks, Gloucester* (correspondence, 1932, Arkell Museum curatorial files).

2. For instance, *List of Vessels Belonging to the District of Gloucester* (Gloucester, Mass.: John Rogers, 1874), 12–13, lists the ships and crew lost in August 1873. D. Scott Atkinson, "Winslow Homer in Gloucester: Hymns to an Older America," in D. Scott Atkinson and Jochen Wierich, *Winslow Homer in Gloucester* (Chicago: Terra Museum of American Art, 1990), 25–26, discusses the dangers of fishing, Homer's probable presence in Gloucester at the time of a terrible storm, and the meaning of *Waiting for Dad*.

5 WOMAN ON THE BEACH, MARSHFIELD 1874

Watercolor over graphite on wove paper, 7 3/16 x 13 7/8 inches
Inscribed LR: Homer/74
Arkell Museum at Canajoharie, Gift of Bartlett Arkell, 1941
317113 (GG 490)

Provenance: Charles S. Homer Jr., by bequest, 1910; Mrs. Charles S. Homer Jr., by bequest, 1917; Arthur P. Homer, by bequest, 1937; Mrs. Arthur P. Homer, by bequest, 1940; (William Macbeth, Inc., 1941); Bartlett Arkell, 1941

WOMAN ON THE BEACH, MARSHFIELD is one of Homer's numerous contributions to a popular theme of his time: fashionable young women promenading at the seaside as an expression of longing and romantic possibility. As an illustrator, Homer pictured young women at beaches for magazines like *Harper's Weekly*. *On the Beach— Two Are Company, Three Are None*, for instance, which *Harper's* published on August 17, 1872, makes romance the explicit subject. The elegantly dressed figure in *Woman on the Beach, Marshfield* forms a striking silhouette in her black dress and bright red shawl. She walks alone on an empty beach and raises her hand as if looking out to sea, injecting a note of mystery. Homer repeated the watercolor's concept and setting for several later works featuring two women on a beach. These include the watercolor *Evening on the Beach* of about 1878 (Colby College Museum of Art, Waterville, Me.) and the oil painting *By the Sea Side* of 1880 (Michele & Donald D'Amour Museum of Fine Arts, Springfield, Mass.).

Homer based *Woman on the Beach, Marshfield* on a detailed drawing he made in 1873 (private collection).[1] He spent much of the summer of 1873 in Gloucester, on the shore north of Boston, but he could have gone elsewhere, including Marshfield, on the coast south of Boston.[2] Homer imparted a degree of finish to this watercolor, incorporating such details as small stones or shells scattered across the beach to break up the flatness of the sand. *Woman on the Beach, Marshfield* represents the type of proven-subject watercolor Homer painted in his studio with the hopes of selling. The following year, he decided to stop working as an illustrator and earn his living through his watercolors. MH

NOTES

1. GG, Record II, 257, 271; illustrated.

2. GG, Record II, 271, discusses the possibility that Homer's family identified the work's setting as Marshfield. Homer's descendants owned the watercolor until Macbeth Gallery sold it to Bartlett Arkell in 1941 as *On the Beach at Marshfield* (GG, Record II, 271, and Macbeth Gallery records, 1838–1968, bulk 1892–1953, Archives of American Art, Smithsonian Institution, Box 112, reel 2822).

6 HOMEWORK 1874

Watercolor over graphite on wove paper, 8¼ x 4¹⁵⁄₁₆ inches
LL: Homer/74
Arkell Museum at Canajoharie, Gift of Bartlett Arkell, 1940
317102 (GG 511)

Provenance: Charles S. Homer Jr., by bequest, 1910; Mrs. Charles S. Homer Jr., by bequest 1917; Arthur P. and Charles L. Homer, by bequest, 1937; (William Macbeth, Inc., ca. 1938); Bartlett Arkell, 1939, for the Canajoharie Library and Art Gallery

BETWEEN 1871 AND 1875, Homer drew and painted a number of works that depict children reading. In them he expressed, usually with a touch of humor, both the importance of education and the current idealization of country childhood. In addition to *Homework*, these works include *The Country School* of 1871 (Saint Louis Art Museum) and *The Noon Recess* of 1873 (Warner Collection, Tuscaloosa), both oil paintings of schoolroom interiors.[1] The theme of *The Noon Recess*, which features a lone boy presumably kept inside to finish his work, is similar to that of *Homework*.

The watercolor's flat patterns and contrasts of light and dark would suit it to reproduction in a wood engraving, Homer's financial mainstay at the time. The reader in *Homework* is surrounded by the emphatic geometry of wall moldings, window frame, and desk. As much as the boy is engrossed in his task, certain details imply that he is longing to be outside. The open window is an obvious reference to the outdoors, as is the sunlight that falls on his shirt and chair. The sun also creates a rectangular patch on the floor, which casts reflected light on the boy's toes and the chair rung. These areas in turn call attention to his bare feet, demonstrating his country origins, and to his hat trapped under the chair. The hat, while relieving the straight lines of the desk and chair, suggests that the boy is similarly trapped.

Other elements give the impression of an actual place and soften the grid: the desk and chair sit at a slight angle to the wall, a string hangs down from the window shade, a slanted stick holds up the window, and flowers decorate the Hitchcock chair. This delicate chair, a popular type for domestic interiors, most likely means the setting is a country home. The schoolroom furniture featured in Homer's oil paintings consists of long, sturdy wooden benches and tables with slanted tops.

Homer's compression of forms in a shallow space resulted in a bold design. He painted with considerable care, applying transparent washes with white opaque highlights and repeating shades of brown and blue.[2] The level of detail and finish suggests this was a studio piece intended for sale. MH

NOTES

1. Nicolai Cikovsky Jr. and Franklin Kelly, *Winslow Homer* (Washington, D.C.: National Gallery of Art, 1995), 88–90, discusses Homer's paintings of the country school. On additional works, see GG, Record II, 367, for an illustration of *Reading at Her Desk* (private collection), a charcoal drawing heightened with white and dated 1875, which shares the theme but not the composition of *Homework*, and Record II, 294, for the charcoal with watercolor *Girls at a Window*, 1874, which resembles *Homework* in setting. *Homework* entered the Bartlett Arkell collection under that title.

2. Lesley Paisley, Williamstown Art Conservation Center examination report, December 2013, Arkell Museum curatorial files, indicates that Homer used careful lifting with a fine brush to achieve the light areas of toes and window-shade string, and that some fading of bluish green has occurred in the back wall.

7 THE ROOSTER (Rooster) 1874

Oil on canvas, 21 3/8 x 20 1/8 inches
Inscribed LR: HOMER (under this signature is a smaller one: Homer '74)
Arkell Museum at Canajoharie, Gift of Bartlett Arkell, 1945
317109 (GG 558)

Provenance: Charles S. Homer Jr., by bequest, 1910; (William Macbeth, Inc., 1912); Robert Sterling Clark, New York, 1915 (William Macbeth, Inc., 1944); Bartlett Arkell, 1945, for the Canajoharie Library and Art Gallery

A PORTRAIT of a rooster might appear to be an unusual subject for Winslow Homer, but he did include roosters in other farmyard scenes. Homer exhibited a watercolor of a very similar rooster, titled *Shoo!*, at the Century Association on March 6, 1875 (Addison Gallery of American Art, Andover, Mass.), now also known as *The Rooster*.[1] *Shoo!*'s rooster, however, is running across a landscape setting, while the Arkell's is a portrait of the bird posed against a green background, without any clues to location or setting. Homer's close-up profile view of the rooster suggests some knowledge of the colorful chromolithographic depictions of fowl found in such contemporary publications as Lewis Wright's *Illustrated Book of Poultry* of 1873. These images usually include the birds' environment of earth and grass, as well as a ground-level view of farm buildings. But during the 1870s there were also many illustrated journals that showed profile views of poultry, usually in black and white, without any background setting.

The virtually square shape of the canvas of *The Rooster* is unusual for Homer, but it is the shape of tiles he painted in the late 1870s. His eight-inch square ceramic tile entitled *Morning* depicts a rooster in profile that is similar in pose and coloring to the Arkell rooster, with the notable exception that this rooster perches on top of a globe of the world. The exact date of the rooster tile is unknown. Homer's earliest known tiles date from 1877, the year he joined an informal group of artists called the Tile Club. The group met in each other's studios to socialize and enjoy food, drink, and tobacco while decorating ceramic tiles provided by the evening's host. Homer's tiles were often more colorful and detailed than some of the members' more monochromatic tiles, indicating that Homer took the production of his tiles seriously and may have produced some outside the gatherings of the club.

The correspondence between the tile version of Homer's rooster and the painted one invites speculation that he used the painting as inspiration for the tile. At some point Homer added a new signature on the painting in extraordinarily large letters, covering his earlier signature and a date of 1874. He may have re-signed the painting while preparing it to be exhibited at the Century Association in April 1876, or he could have created this large signature when he was reviewing, and perhaps reworking, the painting as he was planning the tile that was probably completed in 1878.[2] DEF

NOTES

1. GG, Record II, 350–51, cites "City Intelligence, Art at the Century," *New York Evening Post*, March 8, 1875, to identify and date *The Rooster* in the Addison Gallery of American Art as *Shoo!* 1875.

2. GG, Record II, 351–52; the tile *Morning* is illustrated in GG, Record III, 94–95.

8 MOONLIGHT 1874

Watercolor over graphite on wove paper, 13 7/8 x 20 11/16 inches
Inscribed LL: Winslow Homer 1874
Verso: faint pencil sketch of two seated boys
Arkell Museum at Canajoharie, Gift of Bartlett Arkell, 1941
317103 (GG 529)

Provenance: Charles S. Homer Jr., by bequest, 1910; Mrs. Charles S. Homer Jr., by bequest, 1917; Arthur P. and Charles L. Homer, by bequest, 1937; (William Macbeth, Inc., 1938); Bartlett Arkell, 1940

MOONLIGHT **WAS PROBABLY** included in an exhibition of the American Society of Painters in Water Colors, held at the galleries of the Brooklyn Art Association, under the title *East Hampton Beach*[1] and described in the *New York Evening Post* on March 8, 1875:

Winslow Homer contributes, as usual, a multitude of drawings, some of which are mere indications of form and color, while others are finished pictures. One of the latter works gives

a view on the "East Hampton Beach at Twilight," or rather at early moonrise. The moon is just rising above the horizon, and casts a broad mass of light over the surface of the water, and against the brilliant illumination the figures of a loving couple seated upon the sands are drawn in bold relief. The subject is sensational but very effective in its way.[2]

Twilight, and the ocean lit by the moon, appear in other works by Homer, but the actual depiction of the moon is rare in his art. He did show the moon in several of his 1880 watercolors of schooners, such as *Eastern Point Light* (Princeton University Art Museum). He also created a few oil paintings depicting a moon, rather than just the light of the moon on the water, but these works are not about

20. Winslow Homer (1836–1910)
Three Boys in a Dory with Lobster Pots, 1875
Watercolor and gouache over graphite on paper, 13 9/16 x 20 1/4 inches. The Nelson-Atkins Museum of Art, Kansas City, Missouri, Purchase: William Rockhill Nelson Trust, 44-55/1

21. Detail of reverse of *Moonlight* with sketch of two boys, ca. 1874. Graphite on wove paper

couples on the beach; thus, *Moonlight* stands out as an unusual and noteworthy theme for Homer.[3]

Although Homer did not portray a couple under the moon in any other paintings, he did depict this theme in an engraved illustration, and repeated the engraved couple on a painted ceramic tile. *Flirting on the Sea-Shore and on the Meadow*, published in *Harper's Weekly* on September 19, 1874, and *A Littoral Tile* (ca. 1878; Detroit Institute of Arts), show the pair on a beach, looking at each other in conversation, which is quite unlike the couple in *Moonlight*, with the woman facing away from her companion toward the moon and the sea.

Homer began *Moonlight*, as he did most of his watercolors, with a pencil sketch, laying out the composition before adding watercolor.[4] An examination of the backside of the paper reveals a pencil sketch for a completely different work. The two boys in this faint sketch (fig. 21) turn up in the watercolor *Three Boys in a Dory with Lobster Pots* of 1875 (fig. 20). Homer first used this pair of boys in 1873 in both the watercolor *Seven Boys in a Dory* (Farnsworth Art Museum, Rockland, Me.) and the oil painting *Three Boys in a Dory* (private collection). DEF

NOTES

1. See GG, Record II, 311–12.

2. As quoted in GG, Record II, 321.

3. Homer oil paintings with a moon include *Searchlight on Harbor Entrance, Santiago de Cuba* (1901; Metropolitan Museum of Art), and the painting of fishermen in the ocean called *Kissing the Moon* (1904; Addison Gallery of American Art, Phillips Academy, Andover, Mass.).

4. Leslie Paisley, Williamstown Art Conservation Center, Examination Report, December 2013, Arkell Museum curatorial files. Paisley records Homer's method: beginning with a pencil sketch, followed by colored washes, followed by opaque media for the figures. This work has some white specks, also found on other works by Homer, which conservators believe to be residues of a resist, as discussed by Judith Walsh in Martha Tedeschi and Kristi Dahm, *Watercolors by Winslow Homer: The Color of Light* (New Haven: Yale University Press, 2008), 162.

9 CONTRABAND 1875

Watercolor over graphite on wove paper, 8 15/16 x 7 3/4 inches
Inscribed LL: Homer 75
Arkell Museum at Canajoharie, Gift of Bartlett Arkell, 1937
317101 (GG 587)

Provenance: Edward Delano, New York, n.d.;
Joseph F. Hitch, Brooklyn, his cousin, 1881; Mrs.
M. R. Brownell, Fairhaven, Mass., his daughter;
(William Macbeth, Inc., 1937); Bartlett Arkell, 1937

THE TITLE of this work ensures that it will be understood in the context of the Civil War, though Homer painted it ten years after the war ended. The African American child is the contraband, a term applied to escaped slaves seeking refuge behind Northern lines. The man wears the distinctive jacket and cap of a Union army Zouave regiment. Homer may have intended to mark the war's anniversary, since *Contraband* is emblematic in composition and symbolic in details. The figures sit facing each other against a plain background. Their limbs echo each other's, and their knees and feet touch. The soldier appears to offer the boy a drink from his canteen, which is placed prominently between them and held by one black hand and one white hand. The image presents a clear message of sympathy and unity during the turmoil of the Reconstruction era.

American Zouaves derived their colorful costume from earlier North African Zouave fighters. Homer represented Zouave soldiers at the time of the Civil War but did not include them in the few Civil War subjects he painted in the early 1870s. In 1875 he returned to the subject twice: *Contraband* and the oil painting *Foraging Party of Duryea's Zouaves*, which is known today from reviewers' descriptions.[1] Except for *Contraband*, Homer pictured all of his Zouaves in the blue cropped jacket, baggy red pants, red sash, white gaiters, and red fez-like hat typical of the Duryea unit. *Contraband's* figure wears the trimmer, more practical blue pants and calf-length boots of a regular Union soldier. Though the uniform varied in reality, Homer's color choice was likely an artistic one, since red pants might have overwhelmed the boy.[2] Homer paired a mature, experienced Zouave with a young, innocent child. He painted them in contrasting ways as well, using more precise brushwork for the soldier. He gave the boy's face beauty and individuality.

Contraband is one of at least eight works by Homer that feature the same African American youth as model. It is most clearly related to the watercolors *The Busy Bee* (private collection) and *A Flower for the Teacher* (Georgia Museum of Art), both also from 1875 and shown along with *Contraband* in the American Watercolor Society annual exhibition of 1876. In all three watercolors, the child is dressed in the same tattered clothing: white shirt, tan vest, and patched pants. He is also similarly posed—in profile or near profile view. Recent scholars have concluded that Homer painted these works during his summer in the country or in his New York studio, using a model he found in either place—not as the result of a visit to the South.[3] MH

NOTES

1. On Homer's war subjects from the early 1870s and *Foraging Party of Duryea's Zouaves*, see GG, Record II, 284, 392–93.

2. One prominent unit wore baggy blue pants: Hawkins's Zouaves of New York City. Their leader, Rush Hawkins, had become a book and art collector by 1875. According to Marc Simpson, *Winslow Homer: Paintings of the Civil War* (San Francisco: The Fine Arts Museums of San Francisco, 1988), 168, Homer bought a Zouave uniform at the time of the Civil War. As noted in GG, Record II, 382, *Contraband* was sold out of the 1876 American Watercolor Society exhibition.

3. Mary Ann Calo, "Winslow Homer's Visits to Virginia during Reconstruction," *American Art Journal* 12 (Winter 1980): 19; Nicolai Cikovsky Jr. and Franklin Kelly, *Winslow Homer* (Washington, D.C.: National Gallery of Art, 1995), 148; Margaret C. Conrads, *Winslow Homer and the Critics: Forging a National Art in the 1870s* (Princeton, N.J.: Princeton University Press, in association with the Nelson-Atkins Museum of Art, Kansas City, 2001), 88–94; and GG, Record II, 382–86. Homer's one documented return to the South was in 1877 (GG, Record II, 415–19).

10 THE PUMPKIN PATCH (Husking) 1878

Watercolor over graphite on wove paper, 13 5/16 x 20 1/4 inches
Inscribed LR: Homer 1878
Arkell Museum at Canajoharie, Gift of Bartlett Arkell, 1939
317107 (GG 748)

Provenance: Dr. Josiah Gilbert Holland, New York, 1879; Mrs. Bleecker Van Wagener, Alstead Center, NH, his daughter, 1881; Garrat B. Van Wagener, Denver, her son, n.d.; Mrs. Garrat Van Wagener, Denver, 1937; (William Macbeth, Inc., 1938); Bartlett Arkell, 1939

THE PUMPKIN PATCH is a harvest scene, a subject popular with American landscape and genre painters throughout the nineteenth century. Its appeal is obvious in Homer's watercolor, which extols both the beauty and the bounty of nature. The work bore the title *Husking* when Homer sent it to the American Watercolor Society annual exhibition of 1879.[1] Several men or boys in the background presumably husk corn, but their activity is hardly noticeable. At some point before its acquisition by Bartlett Arkell in 1939, the watercolor's title had been changed to reflect the prominence of the pumpkin patch. Pumpkins were commonly planted alongside corn, as seen in the cut stubs of the corn plants amid the pumpkin leaves in the foreground. This combination offered Homer rich color and a variety of round and straight forms. He rendered the tall stalks as a tan mass overlaid by small strokes of golden color lit by the sun; the corn tops shift to a gray tone as the tassels stand out against the blue hills and sky in the distance. The whole is suffused with sunlight. This work demonstrates the variety of watercolor techniques Homer often used, including transparent washes, opaque color, blotting, scraping, and wet lifting.[2]

Homer created similar scenes of corn and pumpkin patches in the same year, as well as both earlier and later in date. The small ink drawing *Pumpkins among the Corn* (Carnegie Museum of Art, Pittsburgh) was intended to illustrate an article titled "Glimpses of New England Farm Life," which *Scribner's Monthly* included in its August 1878 issue.[3] Presumably Homer painted the Arkell Museum's watercolor later that fall, along with another titled *The Pumpkin Patch* (Mead Art Museum, Amherst College), depicting a family standing among pumpkins. *For to Be a Farmer's Boy* (Art Institute of Chicago), a watercolor of 1887, more closely resembles the Arkell's *Pumpkin Patch* in outlining a boy against the horizon. All of these works show Homer's long-term interest in this particular harvest theme and his tendency to reuse favorite compositions.

Following the pattern of many artists of the period, Homer usually traveled from late spring to early fall and found painting motifs in each locale. He seems to have been especially restless, often staying in a number of spots in one season. In 1878, he spent part of the summer at Houghton Farm in Mountainville, New York (see entries 11 and 12). By October, he had most likely moved further north to the area near Leeds, New York, at the edge of the Catskills.[4] MH

NOTES

1. GG, Record III, 172–73, on the work's title and its purchase from the exhibition by Dr. Josiah Gilbert Holland.

2. On Homer's watercolor techniques, see Martha Tedeschi and Kristi Dahm, *Watercolors by Winslow Homer: The Color of Light* (New Haven: Yale University Press, 2008).

3. See GG, Record III, 106–7, on the ink drawing and illustration. See also GG, Record II, 274–75, and Record IV.2, 446, for additional corn and pumpkin scenes.

4. GG, Record III, 16–17; 166–57.

11 LITTLE SHEPHERDESS 1878

Watercolor and graphite on paper laid down on board, 11¾ x 8¾ inches
Inscribed LL: WH. 1878
Cheryl Chase and Stuart Bear
(GG 696)

Provenance: Charles T. Barney, New York, n.d.; Mrs. Charles T. Barney, New York, by 1936; James W. Barney, New York, her son, by 1944; (William Macbeth, Inc., 1944); Bartlett Arkell, New York, 1944; Mrs. Bartlett (Louise) Arkell, New York, by bequest, 1946; Elizabeth Campbell Wilson, New York, her daughter, by bequest, 1970; (Spanierman Gallery, New York, 1999)

THE SHEPHERDESS was a major theme in Winslow Homer's work of 1878–79.[1] *Little Shepherdess* is almost identical to the slightly smaller graphite and gouache drawing *Girl in Sunbonnet* (Crystal Bridges Museum of American Art, Bentonville, Ark.). In both of these works, Homer placed the young shepherdess on the top of a hill, with clouds billowing behind. *Little Shepherdess*, however, is painted in a full range of colors and portrays more sky, with two birds in the distance.

No sheep appear in either of these works, but the girl is identifiable as a shepherdess by the staff placed across her lap. This is not the eighteenth-century image of a fancifully costumed shepherdess, which Homer was also portraying at the time in such watercolors as *Bo-Peep*, 1878 (Museum of Fine Arts, Boston).[2] The little shepherdess wears a sunbonnet and is dressed for work on the farm. Similar bonneted country girls appear in Homer's works created at Houghton Farm, located near Mountainville, New York, and also at other farms and rural sites in New York and New England during the 1870s.

The sparse landscape of sky and hilltop does not offer any landmarks to indicate a specific location. But it is known that Homer spent time at Houghton Farm in the spring, summer, and fall of 1878, and a contemporary account noted, "On either side of the farm the land rises rapidly into hills."[3] The date of the work and the combination of hillside and bonneted shepherdess make Houghton Farm the most likely location for this watercolor.

The *Little Shepherdess* was purchased by Bartlett Arkell in 1944. He died two years later, and the work remained in the Arkell family until 1970. DEF

NOTES

1. GG, Record III, includes over fifty works by Homer from 1877 to 1880 depicting a shepherdess. This number includes tiles, drawings, watercolors, and oil paintings. Most of these date from 1878 to 1879.

2. For a discussion on Houghton Farm and Homer's Bo-Peep and peasant shepherdesses, see Helen A. Cooper, *Winslow Homer Watercolors* (New Haven: Yale University Press, in association with the National Gallery of Art, 1986), 52–65; Sarah Burns, "The Pastoral Ideal: Winslow Homer's Bucolic America," in Barbara Bloemink et. al., *Frederic Church, Winslow Homer and Thomas Moran: Tourism and the American Landscape* (New York, Boston: Cooper-Hewitt Design Museum, 2006), 119–31; and David Tatham, "Winslow Homer and Houghton Farm," in David Tatham and David Lake Prince, *Winslow Homer's Empire State: Houghton Farm and Beyond* (Syracuse: Syracuse University Press, 2009), 39–45.

3. D. P. Penhallow, "Meteorology," *Houghton Farm Experiment Department Series*, I, no. 1, 1882, 8.

12 SHEPHERDESS AND SHEEP ca. 1878

Oil on canvas, 15 ½ x 22 ½ inches
Inscribed verso: "...re Picture of Value"
Arkell Museum at Canajoharie, Gift of Bartlett Arkell, 1942
317110 (GG 754)

13 GIRL AT THE FENCE ca. 1878

Oil on canvas, 15 ½ x 22 ¾ inches
Arkell Museum at Canajoharie, Gift of Bartlett Arkell, 1942
317274 (GG 755)

Provenance: Charles S. Homer Jr., by bequest, 1910; Mrs. Charles S. Homer Jr., by bequest, 1917; Carnegie Institute, Pittsburgh, by gift, 1918; (Downtown Gallery, 1941); (E.C. Babcock Galleries, 1941); (William Macbeth, Inc., 1942); Bartlett Arkell, 1942

WINSLOW HOMER explored the image of a shepherdess in numerous watercolors in the late 1870s, but *Shepherdess and Sheep* is one of only five known oil paintings on this theme. Homer's depiction of the subject varied from farm girl to playful Bo-Peep to the heroic costumed Bo-Peep in *Spring: The Shepherdess of Houghton Farm* (1879; private collection).[1] The Arkell shepherdess is probably from Houghton Farm, but in her pose and attire she stands as the antithesis of the bold young woman in *Spring: The Shepherdess of Houghton Farm*. The Arkell's shepherdess wears the same working attire as the girl in *The Shepherdess* (1879; private collection).[2] This latter painting was originally owned by Lawson Valentine, the proprietor of Houghton Farm, near Mountainville, New York, where Homer visited in the late 1870s. The Valentines had known the artist since he was a young boy, and they supported his early career by purchasing many of his farm-themed works, including images of both the working and the Bo-Peep types of shepherdesses.[3]

Valentine purchased Houghton Farm in 1876 as a summer retreat from the city and a place to advance modern scientific ideas about farming.

He hired Henry Alvord in 1881 as his general manager, and in June 1882 Alvord observed that "near the southern boundary of the farm, are the houses of the farmer and the shepherd, and also the large sheep barn."[4] This description dates from a few years after Homer was at Houghton Farm, but it is noteworthy that it refers to a shepherd, a familiar male occupation. There are no men tending sheep in Homer's paintings because the artist was not merely painting what and who he saw on the farm—he was selecting views and models to present the ideal view of country life that appealed to his urban patrons.

The shepherdess was a popular image in European paintings—Homer could have found inspiration for his costumed Bo-Peeps and peasant shepherdesses in works by other artists. He was credited in his time, however, for presenting a distinctly American shepherdess. A few years after this painting was completed, art critic George Sheldon wrote, "Mr. Homer appears with one of those admirable young. . . . A 'Shepherdess' we have called her—not the Swiss shepherdess who sits on her alpenstock as if it were a high chair, and knits stockings with a face heavy and heartless, destitute of aspirations and blank hymeneally, but the American shepherdess, . . . where graze her father's sheep, whom she is tending with more or less competency, speaks of subdued, honest, and active day-dreams. Millet never knew her."[5] Sheldon was declaring Homer's distance from Jean-François Millet's peasant shepherdesses,

but more recent Homer scholars have noted this French artist's influence on Homer's work.[6] The Arkell's *Shepherdess and Sheep* has features akin to the work of Millet and other Barbizon artists. The bearing of the shepherdess, with her head bowed, recalls the dignity and calm of Millet's *Shepherdess and Her Flock* (Musée d'Orsay, Paris), exhibited to great acclaim at the Paris Salon of 1864. Homer was aware of Millet and the Barbizon artists, who exhibited in Boston during the 1860s, and when he traveled to France in 1867, he painted farm women and stayed at Cerney-la-ville, where Barbizon artists Camille Corot and

Charles-François Daubigny had painted. Homer did not, however, share Millet's religious sentiments, and it would be a mistake to interpret any of Homer's farm workers with the same religious connotation.

Whereas Millet's shepherdess is knitting, Homer's shepherdess is not engaged in any work. She merely holds a staff and drapes her bonnet over her wrist, looking downward in thought or repose, without any apparent obligation to tend to the sheep. The role of tending sheep combined with this tranquil pose and landscape is the personification of a pastoral ideal of easy country life in contrast to complex city life.[7] This idealized view of farm life, without hard work, was a popular theme in paintings by other American artists at the time, such as J. G. Brown and Eastman Johnson.

Shepherdess and Sheep was sent out for conservation in 1969, and it was discovered at that time that there was a second painted canvas on the same stretcher.[8] The long-hidden painting depicts a young woman with her back to the viewer, wearing a white bonnet and a white apron tied over a pink dress. She stands next to a modest wooden farm building, perhaps a pigsty, and looks over a fence at the unseen farm animals. This canvas, now titled *Girl at the Fence*, is not signed or dated, and may have been painted the same year or several years earlier than *Shepherdess and Sheep*. Its subject is unlike Homer's other groupings of figures by a fence, and in contrast to themes such as the shepherdess, it is not repeated or re-created in any other drawings, watercolors, or paintings. DEF

NOTES

1. Illustrated in GG, Record III, 199.

2. Illustrated in GG, Record III, 195.

3. For a discussion of Homer's relationship to Houghton Farm and his drawings, watercolors, and oil paintings of shepherdesses, see Lloyd Goodrich, *Winslow Homer* (New York: Macmillan, in association with the Whitney Museum of American Art, 1944), 62–64; Helen A. Cooper, *Winslow Homer Watercolors* (New Haven: Yale University Press, in association with the National Gallery of Art, 1986), 52–65; and David Tatham, "Winslow Homer and Houghton Farm," in David Tatham and David Lake Prince, *Winslow Homer's Empire State: Houghton Farm and Beyond* (Syracuse: Syracuse University Art Galleries, 2009), 25–45.

4. Henry E. Alvord, "Houghton Farm," in *Houghton Farm Experiment Department* (Newburgh, N.Y.: Ritchie & Hull, 1882), 3–4.

5. George Sheldon, "Sketches and Studies," *Art Journal* 6 (November 1880): 326.

6. Art historians who have discussed Millet's influence on Homer, while also showing the ways Homer's work differed from that of Millet and other Barbizon artists, include Cooper, *Winslow Homer Watercolors*, 52–65; Erica E. Hirshler, "North Atlantic Drift: A Meditation on Winslow Homer and French Painting," in *Weatherbeaten: Winslow Homer and Maine*, ed. Thomas A. Denenberg (New Haven: Yale University Press, in association with the Portland Museum of Art, Maine, 2012), 71–83; and Sarah Burns, *Pastoral Inventions: Rural Life in Nineteenth-Century American Art and Culture* (Philadelphia: Temple University Press, 1989), 214–26.

7. See Sarah Burns, "The Pastoral Ideal: Winslow Homer's Bucolic America," in Barbara Bloemink et. al., *Frederic Church, Winslow Homer and Thomas Moran: Tourism and the American Landscape* (New York, Boston: Cooper-Hewitt Design Museum, 2006), 119–31, for a discussion of how Homer's shepherdess appealed to contemporary tastes for rustic and country life as a respite from urban growth and filth. She also links the shepherdess with the Colonial Revival period as part of the nostalgia for earlier times both "generic and evocative rather than particular."

8. Conservators Sheldon and Caroline Keck's report to the Canajoharie Library (1969) states that "GIRL WITH SHEEP was never off this stretcher, and no one of the several hands that treatment [sic] that painting ever suspected the GIRL AT THE FENCE was concealed beneath."

14 HOUSES ON A HILLSIDE (Houses on a Hill) 1879

Oil on canvas, 15¾ x 22½ inches
Inscribed LR: Homer 1879
Collection of Marie and Hugh Halff, Jr.
(GG 864)

Provenance: Charles S. Homer Jr., by bequest, 1910; Mrs. Charles S. Homer Jr., by bequest, 1917; Arthur P. and Charles L. Homer, by bequest, 1937; (William Macbeth, Inc., 1938); Bartlett Arkell, 1940; Mrs. Bartlett (Louise) Arkell, New York, n.d.; Elizabeth Campbell Wilson, Manchester, Vt., her daughter, n.d.; (James Maroney, Inc., 1978); Steve Martin, Beverly Hills, n.d.; (Christie's, New York, 1985)

HOMER OFTEN PAINTED and sketched female figures on a hillside as a primary subject, but in this work, the girl is barely noticeable. The hillside, the greenery, and the homes are the artist's main interest. The painting, dated 1879, follows a year in which Homer created many watercolors and drawings of sunbonneted girls sitting on a hill, so he had a ready inventory of similar figure types available for quick inclusion in this painting without the need of a model. Most of his images of girls with bonnets sitting on a hill were from Houghton Farm in New York.

The location depicted in *Houses on a Hillside*, however, remains a mystery. During the summer of 1879, Homer visited Houghton Farm but also spent time in West Townsend, Massachusetts, and perhaps in Maine or Pennsylvania.[1] He kept his summer travel plans from the public that year, and it was reported in *Art Amateur* that "Winslow Homer does not as yet care to tell his summer resort."[2] When he returned to New York City in the fall, another reporter noted that his studio "presents an almost deserted appearance as its owner has only today entered it, but having been 'all around' during the summer."[3]

Reminiscent of *Little Shepherdess*, 1878 (see entry 11), the clouds billow against a blue sky. Here the oil paint adds texture and form to the clouds in a manner that foreshadows Homer's treatment of the crashing wave in his painting *Watching the Breakers—A High Sea*, 1896 (see entry 22). DEF

NOTES

1. See the chronology in GG, Record III, 20, 266–67, and by Charles Brock in Nicolai Cikovsky Jr. and Franklin Kelly *Winslow Homer* (Washington, D.C.: National Gallery of Art, 1995), 395.

2. "Summer Haunts of Artists," *Art Amateur* 1 (August 1879): 50, quoted in GG, Record III, 20–21.

3. "Bits of Gossip about the Artists," *New York World*, October 9, 1879, quoted in GG, Record III, 21.

15 SAILING OUT OF GLOUCESTER ca. 1880

Watercolor over graphite on wove paper, 13 11/16 x 19 7/8 inches
Inscribed LR: Homer
Arkell Museum at Canajoharie, Gift of Bartlett Arkell, 1940
317111 (GG 882)

Provenance: Edward C. Stedman, New York, n.d.; Dr. Alexander C. Humphreys, 1905; (American Art Association, Feb. 15, 1917, Humphreys sale, no. 117); (M. Knoedler & Co., 1917); Samuel A. Lewisohn, New York, 1917; (William Macbeth, Inc., 1938); Bartlett Arkell, 1940

HOMER SPENT JULY and August of 1880 in Gloucester, Massachusetts. During his first Gloucester stay, in the summer of 1873, he had depicted children playing by the water and in small boats. He still turned to these scenes in his watercolors of 1880, but he gave ships greater prominence; at times they are the sole subject. Homer almost always featured schooners, usually under sail in groups and often dotting the horizon. He seemed drawn to the striking silhouette of their overall triangular shapes and the varying patterns formed by the set of their sails. These were mostly working vessels—fishing schooners, the backbone of Gloucester's main industry.

Sailing Out of Gloucester differs from the other watercolors from this summer in ways that suggest that Homer knew the boat's owner personally. It pictures a sloop (one mast), not a schooner (two masts). Homer only occasionally represented a sloop, or any single sailboat in such detail, and he rarely chose a view of the stern. The vessel has been identified as most likely the *Kulinda*, a sloop yacht belonging to local resident George J. Marsh.[1]

An avid sailor, Marsh was almost the same age as Homer and also a bachelor. A visitor to Marsh's seaside home in Annisquam described seeing sailing equipment everywhere but also artwork, "pictures" by Homer as well as by two Boston artists, J. Foxcroft Cole and J. Appleton Brown, all of them "tributes given to Mr. Marsh by his artist friends."[2] Marsh worked for many

years as treasurer of the Cape Ann Savings Bank in Gloucester. Two Homer watercolors once hung in the bank: *Sketch of Mr. Marsh at the Tiller of His Sailboat Off Cape Ann*, a close-up view dated 1880 (Indianapolis Museum of Art), and *The Sloop Kulinda*, a bow-on view of a yacht under sail (Carnegie Museum of Art, Pittsburgh).[3]

Sailing Out of Gloucester is nearly identical to two additional Homer watercolors: *Yachting*, dated 1880, and *A Yacht*, undated (both in private collections).[4] In all three works, seas are moderate, and the vessel heels over just enough to show off the graceful curved line of her stern. Homer carefully observed specific nautical features: gaff rig, accurate rigging lines, and wooden hoops around the mast. *Sailing Out of Gloucester* is the most elaborate and likely the last executed of these versions. Clouds and water are more active—and actively brushed—and a female passenger now leans against the mast. A blue pennant at the top of the mast repeats the blue strokes of the water. Gray skies hint at possible stormy weather. On the horizon at the right, there is a schooner instead of a distant spit of land. At the left, the horizon has been obscured. Highly visible rigging lines form a delicate tracery, as do the faint parallel lines marking the cloth strips of the sail. With these details, Homer put the boat on the open sea and conveyed man's fragility in nature. MH

NOTES

1. On the identification of the sailboat, see GG, Record III, 280. Marsh owned two successive sloops named *Kulinda*. The first, built for him in 1876 ("Off-Hand Local Jottings," *Cape Ann Advertiser*, May 26, 1876), measured between 22 and 28 feet in length along the water line ("Cape Ann Yacht Club," *New York Clipper*, August 12, 1881–82). He had the second one built in 1890. Homer focused on another single vessel in his detailed drawing (and related watercolor) of William B. Astor's schooner *Ambassadress* as it appeared in Gloucester Harbor in August 1880 (Cape Ann Museum, Gloucester;

Addison Gallery of American Art, Andover, Mass.). He also sent a work titled *The Yacht Hope* (unlocated) to the 1881 American Watercolor Society annual exhibition.

2. "Bank All Right," *Boston Herald*, October 10, 1896. Marsh lived a colorful, unconventional life, capped by a dramatic death by suicide in 1896 as news of his speculation with trust monies became public.

3. GG, Record III, 278–79, illustrates the two works and describes Lloyd Goodrich's 1940 correspondence with a bank associate. "Was Treasurer Marsh Insane?" *Boston Herald*, October 9, 1896, describes Marsh's involvement in a recent remodeling of the bank, with the result that "many works of art and enviable pieces of antiquity found their way into the room."

4. Homer brought *A Yacht* back to New York. *Yachting* probably remained in Annisquam, since its earliest recorded owners lived there. See GG, Record III, 280-83, for provenance information and illustration of both works, as well as two others from 1880 by Homer that include a partial view of the same boat in the distance. GG, Record III, 280, traces the provenance of *Sailing Out of Gloucester* as far back as Edward C. Stedman of New York, from whom Dr. Alexander C. Humphreys purchased the work in 1905 (as cited in the sale catalogue *The Very Notable Dr. Alexander C. Humphreys Collection, American Art Association*, February 15, 1917, lot 117). "Art Notes. Dr. A. C. Humphrey's Collection of American Pictures," *New York Times*, February 11, 1917, identifies the former owner as Edmund C. Stedman, who was a well-known literary figure and banker.

16 ON THE CLIFF 1881

Watercolor over graphite on wove paper, 13 ½ x 19 inches
Inscribed LL: Homer 1881
Arkell Museum at Canajoharie, Gift of Bartlett Arkell, 1941
317106 (GG 1026)

Provenance: Thomas B. Clarke, New York, n.d.; (American Art Association, Feb. 14–18, 1899, Clarke sale, no. 139); Thomas L. Manson Jr., New York, 1899; (C.W. Kraushaar, by 1918); (M. Knoedler & Co., 1918); (Howard Young Galleries, 1918); Frank K.M. Rehn, by 1922; Duncan Phillips, Washington, D.C., 1922; (Ferargil Galleries, 1940); (William Macbeth, Inc., 1940); Bartlett Arkell, 1940

ON THE CLIFF was created in Tynemouth North Point, near the fishing village of Cullercoats, England.[1] The young women of this region on the North Sea coast became Homer's primary subjects from the summer of 1881 until early November 1882. A man who knew Homer at the time recalled years later that the artist had explained his interest in Cullercoats with these words: "Look at the fisher-girls . . . in the picture I am painting; there are none like them in my country in dress, feature or form."[2]

On the Cliff depicts young women and children on the rock face looking out to sea. There is a ship in the distance at the low horizon line. Homer created other versions of this subject with different numbers of women and children, and he sometimes used other locations along the coast near Cullercoats. *Girl Carrying a Basket* (National Gallery of Art, Washington, D.C.) and *Girls on a Cliff* (Museum of Fine Arts, Boston) have been identified as portraying the same location as *On the Cliff*. But other watercolors showing women and children similar to *On the Cliff*, such as *Fisherman's Family* (Museum of Fine Arts, Boston) and *Under the Cliff, Cullercoats* (Addison Gallery of American Art, Andover, Mass.), depict settings further north from Tynemouth North Point.[3]

In 1882, Homer's Boston dealer organized a successful exhibition of his Cullercoats watercolors, which were well received and praised as "spontaneous" and "delightful" and "redolent of bracing seabreezes. . . . The children of the village are now and then depicted in their sober recreations, as for example when they mount a little headland to sit there and look down of the breakers below."[4] Homer was not the first artist to discover the people and landscape of Cullercoats—it was a region already popular with English artists. But Homer was the first to see the women and the coastline around Cullercoats as uniquely hardy and captivating, rather than simply sentimental and picturesque. DEF

NOTES

1. Tony Harrison, *Winslow Homer in England*, rev. ed. (1983; repr., Ocean Park, Me.: Hornby Editions, 2004), 113. *On the Cliff* is a Tynemouth scene, but William H. Gerdts noted that other works had been incorrectly titled as Tynemouth when they actually depict Cullercoats subjects. Gerdts examined a variety of factors that might have led Homer to Cullercoats in 1881 and argued for the time period 1881–82 to be referred to as "The Cullercoats Years" rather than "The Tynemouth Years." See William H. Gerdts, "Winslow Homer in Cullercoats," *Yale University Art Gallery Bulletin* 36, no. 2 (Spring 1977): 18–35.

2. Alan Adamson, a native of Cullercoats who moved on to America, recalled Winslow Homer's words in "The Homer That I Knew," included in Harrison, *Winslow Homer in England*, 36.

3. All locations cited here are as noted in Harrison, *Winslow Homer in England*.

4. Clipping in scrapbook at Bowdoin College Museum of Art, quoted in GG, Record IV.1, 34.

17 ABOVE THE SEA, TYNEMOUTH (Looking for the Boys) ca. 1881 or 1882

Watercolor over graphite on wove paper, 13¼ x 18⁷⁄₁₆ inches
Inscribed LR: To Mr. Long/with comp'ts of/Winslow Homer
Arkell Hall Foundation, 100021
(GG 1138)

Provenance: Gift to William B. Long in 1882 while visting Homer in Cullercoats, England; Grace Long Morgan (Mrs. Charles Morgan), his daughter, 1918; (William Macbeth, Inc., 1936); Mrs. George A. Ball, Muncie, Ind., 1936; (William Macbeth, Inc., 1938); Bartlett Arkell, 1938; Mrs. Bartlett (Lousie) Arkell, by bequest, 1946

THIS WATERCOLOR is inscribed "To Mr. Long with comp't of Winslow Homer." William B. Long was in Cullercoats when he was given this work, which he called *Looking for the Boys*,[1] and his family recalls that he mentioned meeting the fisherman depicted.[2] The watercolors Homer made during his stay in England often featured women looking out to sea; thus, *Looking for the Boys* was a familiar theme for him at the time, though it was unusual for Homer to let a man be the one watching and waiting. The watercolor stayed in the family until 1936, when the Macbeth Gallery sold it to Mrs. George A. Ball with the title *Above the Sea, Tynemouth*, and this title remained when Macbeth sold it to Bartlett Arkell two years later.

William Long worked at Valentine & Company, a manufacturer of paint and varnish in New York City, where Charles S. Homer Jr., Homer's brother, was also employed. Homer wrote to Long at the company in November 1882: "I remember promising that I would write to you when I decided to go home. I shall sail next Saturday."[3] After Homer returned to America, Henry Lawson, who had just taken over as president of Valentine & Company, purchased *The Lookout*, 1882 (Harvard Art Museums/Fogg Museum), which depicts the same fisherman, but this time he is joined by a woman standing behind him, looking out for the boys.

Years after settling in Maine, Homer reworked and repurposed figures and poses from his Cullercoats experience. *Early Evening*, 1881–1907 (Freer Gallery of Art, Washington, D.C.), includes the fisherman, but here he is overshadowed by two young women standing and knitting above him on the rocks. In 1890, Homer secured a new model to modify the Cullercoats fisherman into an "old salt" from Maine in *Cloud Shadows* (1890; Spencer Museum of Art, Kansas).[4] DEF

NOTES

1. Letter from William Long to his daughter Grace, January 18, 1918, states, "Herewith the Winslow Homer letter written by him to me under date of August 4, 1882, from Cullercoats, England where he painted 'Looking for the Boys' and where he presented the painting to me." The letter to Long from Homer is actually dated November 4, 1882. Copies of both letters are in Arkell Museum curatorial files.

2. Discussion with Judith and Charles Morgan on their visit to the Arkell Museum in August 2008; notes in Arkell Museum curatorial files.

3. Letter and envelope from Winslow Homer to William Long, November 4, 1882. Copy in Arkell Museum curatorial files.

4. Philip C. Beam, "Exhibition Checklist," in Phillip Beam et. al., *Winslow Homer in the 1890s: Prout's Neck Observed* (New York: Hudson Hills Press, in association with the Memorial Art Gallery, University of Rochester, 1990), 104, notes that the man "is seated with his back to the viewer, their attitudes symbolizing a harmonious meeting of youth and old age, she in an attractive dress and he in the garb of an old salt." Beam relies on Mrs. Albert Stevens's identification of the sitter as "her uncle, Benjamin Franklin Sanborn."

18 INSIDE THE BAR 1883

Watercolor and graphite on wove paper, 15 ⅛ x 28 ½ inches
Inscribed LR: Homer '83
The Metropolitan Museum of Art, gift of Louise Ryals Arkell in memory of her husband, Bartlett Arkell
(GG 1172)

Provenance: Charles T. Barney, New York, n.d.;
Mrs. Charles T. Barney, New York, by 1944; James
Barney, New York, her son, by 1944; (William
Macbeth, Inc., 1944); Bartlett Arkell, 1944; Mrs.
(Louise) Bartlett Arkell, by bequest, 1946

WHEN *INSIDE THE BAR* was included in the
annual exhibition of the American Watercolor
Society in 1883, it was praised along with Homer's
other works for being "not only . . . the most complete and beautiful things he has yet produced,
but among the most interesting American art has
yet created."[1] Critics were awed by the woman
at the center of *Inside the Bar*, noting that "the
storm wraps her coarse draperies about her with
the closeness and crisp modeling of sculpture,"
and her "stride is magnificent; she is part of the
storm itself."[2]

Inside the Bar began with sketches in graphite
and watercolor that Homer executed while he was
still in the fishing village of Cullercoats, England.
Homer's 1882 study *Storm at Sea* (McNay Art
Museum, San Antonio) established the location
of the rocky coast and boats; and an earlier work
in graphite and gouache, *Windy Day Cullercoats*,

1881 (Portland Museum of Art, Maine), placed
a fisherwoman in the center. Homer used both
studies to create *Inside the Bar* after he had
returned to America.[3]

Bartlett Arkell purchased *Inside the Bar* for
his personal collection in 1944. His wife, Louise,
donated the watercolor to the Metropolitan
Museum of Art in his memory in 1954. DEF

NOTES

1. Mrs. Schuyler van Rensselaer, "An American Artist in England,"
Century 27 (November 1883), 17.

2. *Art Amateur* 8 (March 1881): 81, and "The Water-Color Exhibition," *Harpers' Weekly* 27 (February 2, 1883): 71, quoted in Franklin
Kelly, "A Process of Change," in Nicolai Cikovsky Jr. and Franklin
Kelly, *Winslow Homer* (Washington, D.C.: National Gallery of Art,
1995), 219.

3. Tony Harrison, *Winslow Homer in England*, rev. ed. (1983;
repr., Ocean Park, Me.: Hornby Editions, 2004), 78, illustrates all
three works and identifies their setting as Cullercoats Bay, East
of North Pier.

19 HOMECOMING (Home-Coming, On the Way Home, The Return Home) 1883

Watercolor over graphite on wove paper, 14 7/16 x 21 1/2 inches
Inscribed LL: Winslow Homer 1883
Inscribed verso: "North of England coming ashore"
Arkell Museum at Canajoharie, by bequest, 1946
317116 (GG 1178)

Provenance: Unidentified private collection, n.d.; (Ortgies & Co., Jan. 22, 1896, no. 55, as *On the Way Home*); John Harrison Rhoades, New York, probably 1896; John Harrison Rhoades Jr., New York, probably 1906; (M. Knoedler & Co., 1915); (Henry Reinhardt & Son/Reinhardt Galleries, Chicago & New York, 1915); Ralph Cudney, Chicago, probably 1915; (E.C. Babcock Art Galleries, 1935); (William Macbeth, Inc., 1935); Bartlett Arkell, 1935; Mrs. (Louise) Bartlett Arkell, 1946

WINSLOW HOMER returned from England in November 1882 with unfinished sketches and watercolors, as well as the clear memory of fishermen, their wives, and the children at Cullercoats. *Homecoming* is dated by Homer as 1883, but the reverse of the paper includes the inscription "North of England coming ashore," revealing that the subject came from England and the work was completed in his American studio.[1] Before Homer left England, he wrote to a friend that he had made arrangements to stay at 80 East Washington Avenue in New York City,[2] but he was soon drawn to Maine, where the Homer family summered at Prout's Neck. Homer's father purchased property there in January 1883, and in March Winslow's brother Charles acquired some of the Prout's Neck land and completed the family summer home, known as "the Ark," in time for the family to stay on the property that summer.[3] Like Cullercoats, Prout's Neck has a rocky coastline, and Homer used this setting to return to the subject of fishermen and their families on the ocean shoreline (fig. 22).

Many of the watercolors Homer created at Cullercoats were about watching and waiting for the fishermen to return from the sea. Homer first presented the subject of family looking out at the sea when he was in Gloucester, Massachusetts, in 1873. He continued this theme in Cullercoats. *Homecoming*, begun in England and completed in America, reveals the happy ending both the Cullercoats and Gloucester families longed for.

Bartlett Arkell purchased *Homecoming* in 1935, and a year later allowed it to go back to Winslow Homer's home and studio for the *Century Loan Exhibition as a Memorial to Winslow Homer* in 1936. DEF

22. Photographer unknown
View of the Charles Savage Homer House, the Ark, and Stable from the Eatern Shore, Prout's Neck, Maine, with the Checkley House and Fairbanks Cottage, ca. 1883. Photograph. Bowdoin College Museum of Art, Brunswick, Maine, Gift of the Homer Family, 1964.69.177.22

NOTES

1. It is not clear what "North of England" might mean. In *Winslow Homer in England*, rev. ed. (1983; repr., Ocean Park, Me.: Hornby Editions, 2004), 83, Tony Harrison groups this watercolor with works Homer painted at "Cullercoats Bay, East of North Pier." Examination Record 12/30/2013 by Leslie Paisley, Williamstown Art Conservation Center, Inc., notes the order in which different mediums were added. "The composition was painted quickly, initially most likely out of doors. The composition was laid out with a pencil sketch over which colored transparent washes were applied wet on the dry paper. . . . The technique in the sky involved at least two separate colored washes. Areas of the sky and foreground were blotted after. . . . Applications of opaque colors . . . were added to suggest the figures in the foreground. The opaque media was applied last."

2. Letter and envelope from Winslow Homer to William Long, November 4, 1882. Copy in Arkell Museum curatorial files. His actual address was 80 Washington Square East.

3. Kenyon C. Bolton III, "The Right Place: Winslow Homer and the Development of Prout's Neck," in *Weatherbeaten: Winslow Homer and Maine*, ed. Thomas A. Denenberg (New Haven: Yale University Press, in association with the Portland Museum of Art, Maine, 2012), 32.

20 SPONGE FISHING, BAHAMAS ca. 1885

Watercolor over graphite on wove paper, 14 x 20 1/16 inches
Inscribed LR: Winslow Homer
Arkell Museum at Canajoharie, Gift of Bartlett Arkell, 1940
317112 (GG 1264)

Provenance: Charles S. Homer Jr., by gift of Homer, before 1892; Mrs. Charles S. Homer Jr., by bequest, 1917; Charles L. Homer, by bequest, 1937; (William Macbeth, Inc., 1938); Bartlett Arkell, 1940

IN 1884, HOMER moved permanently to Prout's Neck, Maine, but he spent many winters in warm climates. That December he traveled to Nassau, the capital of the Bahamas, in the company of his father. He stayed for nearly four months, which included a side trip to Cuba.[1] It was a productive time, as he returned home with over thirty watercolors of the Bahamas alone, among them the Arkell's *Sponge Fishing, Bahamas*. Almost two years later, *Century* magazine reproduced nine of the Bahamas subjects to illustrate an article on Nassau, but *Sponge Fishing, Bahamas* was not one of them. By 1892, the work belonged to Homer's brother Charles.[2]

Homer's Bahama watercolors form a complete contrast to the dark, somber works depicting English fisherfolk of several years earlier (see entries 16–19). They capture the brilliant light and strong color of the Caribbean and the physical beauty of its native inhabitants. In many scenes, muscular black men dive for conch, sponge, or coral in the bright blue sea. The crowded boat in *Sponge Fishing, Bahamas* has perhaps stopped to let a passenger dive or has been approached by a swimmer offering a sea creature, a sponge or a conch.[3]

The most striking aspect of *Sponge Fishing, Bahamas* is how freely Homer painted it. Transparent washes and broad strokes indicate sky and water. Passengers remain a loose mass made up of dabs of color, except for the more clearly defined woman seated at the stern. The boat's hull takes shape from reserved areas of the white paper. Despite the work's seemingly rapid execution, its composition is not casual. A vivid blue splotch picks out a man leaning over the side of the boat; his figure breaks up the hull's expanse and intensifies the sunlight. With a few touches of deep color in that area, Homer created a cascade of forms that offsets the woman in white. His other watercolors from his Bahamas trip are equally spontaneous in technique, leading most critics to regard them as sketches but praise them as "unusually notable."[4] On a return visit to the Bahamas in 1898–99, Homer responded once more to color and light and gravitated to similar subject matter. MH

NOTES

1. Helen A. Cooper, *Winslow Homer Watercolors* (New Haven: Yale University Press, in association with the National Gallery of Art, 1986), 130, 144, 146.

2. GG, Record IV.2, 204, 321, discusses the use of Homer's watercolors for the article by William C. Church, "A Midwinter Resort," in *Century* magazine, February 1887. Charles Homer may have assigned the title "Sponge Fishing"; he sent it to an exhibition at the New York Athletic Club in 1892 under that title (Abigail Booth Gerdts, correspondence with the author, November 25, 2013). Macbeth Gallery sold the work to Bartlett Arkell in 1940 as *Sponge Fishing, Bahamas*.

3. *Sponge Fishermen, Bahamas* of ca. 1885 (private collection) shows sponges piled on a wharf for processing. See Cooper, *Winslow Homer Watercolors*, 132, 134, 135, 139, for illustrations of these related works and discussion of the importance and methods of sponge fishing in the Bahamas in Homer's time. Cooper also considers the boat in the Arkell picture to be an island ferry, not a sponge-fishing vessel.

4. *Boston Evening Transcript*, February 25, 1886, cited in Cooper, 147–49.

21 AT TAMPA, FLORIDA (Two Flamingoes, Tampa) 1885

Watercolor over graphite on wove paper, 14 x 19 15/16 inches
Inscribed LL: Homer 85
Inscribed LR: Tampa Fla./1885
Arkell Museum at Canajoharie, Gift of Bartlett Arkell, 1941
31799 (GG 1326)

Provenance: Charles S. Homer Jr., by bequest, 1910; Brooklyn Museum, New York, 1912; Arthur P. and Charles L. Homer, by exchange, 1941; (William Macbeth, Inc., 1941); Bartlett Arkell, 1941

IN 1885, HOMER made his first trip to Florida, again accompanied by his father. The two probably left New York in December. *At Tampa, Florida*, dated 1885, and the watercolor *Spanish Moss at Tampa*, dated 1886 (private collection), identify his whereabouts at the start of his journey. Other views indicate later visits to Key West and Enterprise, Florida. At the end of February, he returned to Jacksonville before heading home, having produced at least a dozen watercolors.[1]

Florida's profuse, exotic foliage impressed Homer most, judging by his concentration on jungle scenes. Whereas in Key West he depicted palm trees, in northern Florida he featured Spanish moss hanging from trees, especially live oaks. *At Tampa, Florida* puts that subject front and center, with half the composition given over to masses of dangling strands. A white egret and a roseate spoonbill in the foreground stand out against the many shades of green and brown. The whole magical scene is a technical tour de force, from the loose, watery jumble of brushstrokes of the foreground foliage to the scraped whites of the birds to the variety of overlays of the moss. The moss is especially striking, as white brushed over green turns to gray against the sky.

Homer sent one or two works from his first Florida winter to the American Watercolor Society's annual exhibitions of 1886, 1887, and 1888. The Arkell Museum's watercolor is most likely the one titled *Tampa, Florida* in the 1888 show. A reviewer described a "jungle scene" in which "Spanish moss drapes the trees and cranes stand contemplative in the marshy reaches."[2] Homer returned to Florida for six more winters. He devoted his time to fishing but also painted in watercolor during two of those occasions. The later works, created in 1890 and 1903–4, feature fishing on inland rivers and on the sea at Key West. They do not recapture his initial thrill at discovering such unusual wild vegetation. MH

NOTES

1. For Homer's itinerary, see Helen A. Cooper, *Winslow Homer Watercolors* (New Haven: Yale University Press, in association with the National Gallery of Art, 1986), 150, 152; Patricia Junker, "Fishing on the St. John's and Homosassa Rivers: Winslow Homer's Florida," in Patricia Junker and Sarah Burns, *Winslow Homer: Artist and Angler* (New York: Thames & Hudson, 2003), 161–83; and GG, Record IV.2, 189–90.

2. "More about the Water Colors," *New York Times*, February 13, 1888, quoted in GG, Record IV.2, 396. Here, also, Abigail Booth Gerdts originally identified *Spanish Moss at Tampa* as the work referred to in this review but has since reassigned the citation to the Arkell's watercolor (correspondence with the author, November 18, 2013).

22 WATCHING THE BREAKERS—A HIGH SEA (High Seas, A High Sea) 1896

Oil on canvas, 24 ¼ x 38 ¼ inches
Inscribed LL: Winslow Homer 1896
Arkell Museum at Canajoharie, Gift of Bartlett Arkell, 1935
317114 (GG 1600)

Provenance: Col. George G. Briggs, Grand Rapids, Mich., 1896; Dr. Frank W. Gunsaulus, Chicago, ca. 1900; (Henry Reinhardt & Son/Reinhardt Galleries, New York & Chicago, ca. 1902); (M. Knoedler & Co., 1902); Grace Rainey (later Mrs. Henry W. Rogers), Cleveland, 1904; (McClees Galleries, Philadelphia, 1919); J. F. Braun, Merion, Penn., 1919; (William Macbeth, Inc., 1932); Stephen C. Clark, New York, 1932; (William Macbeth, Inc., 1935); Bartlett Arkell, 1935[1]

WINSLOW HOMER painted *Watching the Breakers—A High Sea* at his home in Prout's Neck, Maine, in the mid-1890s. More than a decade earlier, Homer had transformed a carriage house at Prout's Neck into his studio and home, and the surrounding views of the shoreline and ocean waves became the focus of his paintings. He often stayed there during the winter months, after the hotels had closed and seasonal residents—including Homer's relatives—had returned to city life.

Winter encouraged the artist's muted palette of whites, green-gray, brown, and black. His cold-season marines, such as *Coast in Winter* (1892; Worcester Art Museum), have no evidence of humankind. But several of his winter scenes in the 1890s include a person or persons—both as a barely noticeable figure among the rocks, as in *Winter Coast* (1890; Philadelphia Art Museum), or central subjects facing out to sea, as in *Below Zero* (1894; Yale University Art Gallery).

In *Watching the Breakers—A High Sea*, three figures (two men in oilskins and a woman with a red scarf) huddle together in the snow, watching an enormous wave crash against the rocks. The people have their backs to the viewer and appear as one silhouetted group rather than as individuals. Homer had employed a similar group of people as one dark mass against a moonlit sea in the painting

Summer Night, 1890 (Musée d'Orsay, Paris). The silhouetted groups in these paintings encourage the viewer to imagine the experience. A contemporary of Homer's conveyed the feeling of *Watching the Breakers—A High Sea* by describing what it would be like to be the woman in the painting: "When the wind blows and the waters roar, purposes are forgotten, individuality is almost lost for a time, and the loiterer becomes scarcely more than a passive, if sentient, portion of the landscape."[2]

Late in 1899, *Watching the Breakers—A High Sea* was compared unfavorably to a "great canvas" recently included in the 1899 exhibition of works belonging to Thomas B. Clarke.[3] The "great canvas" was a winter marine with only shore, sea, and sky. Preferring Homer's unpeopled marines, the critic found fault with Homer's figures in *Summer Night*, calling them awkward, and declared that the artist had found "his highest inspiration in the sea itself."[4] Homer had second thoughts about including people in at least one of his Maine seascapes in 1900. *Northeaster* (1895; Metropolitan Museum of Art) originally included a man on the rocky shore, but Homer painted him out. After so many years of success, it is difficult to believe that Homer would alter or change his paintings because of a critic's comments, but he was always interested in painting works that would please his buying public. *Watching the Breakers—A High Sea* had been sold prior to exhibition and was not available for any revisions, but the owner did not keep the work.

The painting came to M. Knoedler & Co. Gallery in 1902, which sparked a series of letters back and forth between the gallery and Homer about the painting's title and date.[5] Finally, on November 12, 1904, either frustrated over the fact that the painting was still with Knoedler, or just annoyed at the years of correspondence about the painting, Homer wrote, "send that nuisance of a

picture 'High Sea' to Columbus O. or better still to Tacoma Wash. Get it out of sight!"[6]

After Homer's death in 1910, many announcements of his passing listed the painting among his "most notable works,"[7] and from 1911 to the present, *Watching the Breakers—A High Sea* continues to be requested for major retrospective exhibitions and has received praise from art historians, critics, and the public. DEF

NOTES

1. Provenance information was generously provided by Abigail Gerdts from Lloyd Goodrich, edited and expanded by Abigail Booth Gerdts, *Record of Works by Winslow Homer*, vol. V, 1890–1910 (New York: Goodrich-Homer Art Education Project, in press 2014).

2. Unidentified clipping, Bowdoin Scrapbook, February 1892, quoted in Marc Simpson, "You Must Wait, and Wait Patiently," in *Weatherbeaten: Winslow Homer and Maine*, ed. Thomas A. Denenberg (New Haven: Yale University Press, in association with the Portland Museum of Art, Maine, 2012), 106.

3. This reference could be to either *Maine Coast* (Metropolitan Museum of Art) or *Coast in Winter* (Worcester Art Museum). Both are listed in *Private Art Collection of Thomas B. Clarke* (New York: American Art Association, February 1899). *Maine Coast* is described as "one of the artist's finest works, and fully deserves the name of masterpiece."

4. "Pittsburg International Exhibition," *Harper's Weekly* 43 (November 11, 1899): 1149, and repeated in "Fourth Annual Exhibition of the Carnegie Institute, Pittsburgh," *Artist: An Illustrated Monthly Record of Arts and Crafts*, December 1899, 14.

5. There was a great amount of correspondence on this painting between Winslow Homer and its first owner, George Briggs; Homer's dealer, M. Knoedler & Co.; and Carnegie Institute Museum of Art Director John Beatty. Within these letters Homer refers to the painting as "A High Sea" and "High Seas" and dates it to 1894 despite the fact that the painting is clearly inscribed with the date 1896. Correspondence from Winslow Homer about this painting includes: Letter from Winslow Homer to George G. Briggs, February 19, 1896 (Archives of American Art); Letter from Winslow Homer to John Beatty, September 13, 1899, courtesy of Abigail Booth Gerdts from GG, Record V, entry number 1600; Letter from Winslow Homer to M. Knoedler & Co., March 22, 1902, transcribed and illustrated in Marc Simpson, *Winslow Homer: The Clark Collection* (Williamstown, Mass.: Sterling and Francine Clark Art Institute, 2013); Letters owned by Crystal Bridges Museum of American Art (Bentonville, Ark.) including letters from Winslow Homer to M. Knoedler & Co., March 30, 1902, November 9, 1902, and November 12, 1904.

6. Letter from Winslow Homer to M. Knoedler & Co., November 12, 1904 (Crystal Bridges Museum of American Art).

7. Newspapers across the country listed *High Seas* among his "notable works." Samples include "Veteran Artist of Fame Summoned: Winslow Homer Noted for His Pictures of Civil War Scenes, Dead," *Salt Lake Tribune*, October 1, 1910; "Winslow Homer Noted Artist, Dies, Aged 74," *Los Angeles Herald*, October 1, 1910. This painting was not, however, listed at this time in the *New York Times*.

23 FEEDING THE CHICKENS (Barnyard with Boy Feeding Chickens, Boy in a Barnyard)

Oil on paperboard, 12 x 18 ½ inches
Arkell Museum at Canajoharie, Gift of Bartlett Arkell, 1943
317115 (GG 12)

Provenance: Arthur B. Homer, by 1911; Charles L. Homer, by bequest, 1916; (William Macbeth, Inc., 1937); Francis P. Garvan, 1937; (William Macbeth, Inc., 1943); Bartlett Arkell, 1943

WINSLOW HOMER died in 1910. *Feeding the Chickens* belonged to his younger brother, Arthur, by 1911. At that time, Arthur identified the painting as being done by Winslow; the setting as his family's Belmont, Massachusetts, home; and the pictured boy as himself. He also estimated the date to be 1858.[1] Arthur Homer's recollection has led to some confusion, since he was almost sixteen when the family moved to Belmont in 1858, and the boy in the painting looks younger than that.[2] Arthur has a similarly rounded face in Homer's drawing of him dated 1853 (private collection), suggesting that *Feeding the Chickens* may represent Arthur at about that time.[3] Winslow Homer would have been seventeen or eighteen then. His

family lived in Cambridge, and he was just beginning his career as an illustrator. He probably had some instruction from his mother, who painted in watercolor, but in 1855 he started a two-year apprenticeship at Bufford's lithography workshop in Boston. No other Homer paintings from the mid-1850s are known; the first dated oils by him are those from his Civil War period. MH

NOTES

1. GG, Record I, 90–91.

2. GG, Record I, 90, explores this and other issues.

3. Gordon Hendricks, *The Life and Work of Winslow Homer* (New York: Harry N. Abrams, 1979), 21, illustrates the drawing of Arthur and estimates the date of *Feeding the Chickens* to be about 1851. GG, Record I, 88–89, notes that the drawing is inscribed "Portrait of Arthur B. Homer—By Winslow" by a hand other than Homer's, and proposes an approximate date of 1854 for *Feeding the Chickens*. Though the painting went by alternate titles over the years, it was published as *Feeding the Chickens* in William Howe Downes, *The Life and Works of Winslow Homer* (Boston: Houghton Mifflin, 1911), 28, and acquired by Bartlett Arkell under that title.

24 ON THE BATTENKILL

Watercolor over graphite on wove paper, 10⅜ x 14½ inches
Inscribed LR: On the Battenkill Arlington Vt. 18[??]
Arkell Museum at Canajoharie, Gift of Bartlett Arkell, 1940
317104 (GG 376)

Provenance: Charles S. Homer Jr., by bequest, 1910; Mrs. Charles S. Homer Jr., by bequest, 1917; Arthur P. and Charles L. Homer, by bequest, 1937; (William Macbeth, Inc., ca. 1940); Bartlett Arkell, 1940

AN INSCRIPTION in the lower right of this watercolor identifies the site as the Battenkill River in Arlington, Vermont, but the last two numbers of the accompanying date are now illegible. A date of about 1870 has been suggested,[1] which would make this one of Homer's earliest efforts at using the medium other than as a wash to augment a drawing. Arlington is in the Green Mountains, close to the border with New York. The Battenkill, which flows from Vermont into New York to join the Hudson River, was noted for trout fishing. A visit there would have been logical for Homer, who in later life devoted much of his time to fishing and often depicted both rivers and fishing. Homer traveled frequently during the summers. He went to the White Mountains of New Hampshire in 1868 and 1869, and may have passed through Vermont en route and executed this view of the Battenkill. He may also have detoured into Vermont when he made his first visit to the Adirondacks in September 1870.

On the Battenkill represents a summer or perhaps an early fall landscape. Small choppy strokes of green define the bushes, and watery washes create the mountainous background. Liberally applied opaque-white touches highlight the edges of bushes and clouds. The paper, which has darkened over time, is a type found in sketchbooks, rather than one suited to watercolor.[2] MH

NOTES

1. GG, Record II, 12, 138, discusses the history of assigning this date.

2. Lesley Paisley, Williamstown Art Conservation Center examination report, January 2014, Arkell Museum curatorial files.

EXHIBITION HISTORY 1864–1937

Compiled by **Diane E. Forsberg** and **Suzan D. Friedlander**

EXHIBITIONS that included Winslow Homer works purchased by Bartlett Arkell for Canajoharie and his personal collections are listed below from the earliest known exhibition through the Centennial Exhibitions celebrating Winslow Homer's birth. The current title of each work is listed first and the alternate title used in the exhibition is listed second after its catalogue number. Owners at the time of exhibition are listed when known. The exhibition history was compiled from information in the original catalogues in Arkell curatorial files, Macbeth Gallery Records at the Archives of American Art, and the *Record of Works by Winslow Homer* by Lloyd Goodrich, edited and expanded by Abigail Booth Gerdts.

1864 Dodsworth Building, [Artists' Reception], January 1864 [New York]. *In Front of the Guard-House*, owner: The artist

National Academy of Design, *Thirty-ninth Annual Exhibition*, April 15–June 25, 1864 [New York]. *In Front of the Guard-House* (no. 73), owner: The artist

1875 Brooklyn Art Association, *First Annual Exhibition of the American Society of Painters in Water Colors Held at the Galleries of the Brooklyn Art Association*, March 8–20, 1875. *Moonlight* (no. 364, as *East Hampton Beach*; listed as an oil painting), owner: The artist

The Century Association, April 3, 1875 [New York]. *Moonlight*

John Snedecor, New York, and the Haseltine Galleries, Philadelphia, *Spring Exhibition of Fine Works of Art* [auction], exhibited at the Chicago Industrial Exposition Building, late April–May 8, 1875. *Moonlight* (no. 386, as *On the Beach, East Hampton, LI*)

Louisville Industrial Exposition, September 1875. *Moonlight* (no. 166, as *East Hampton Beach*)

Snedecor Gallery, Paintings & Water Colors [auction], November 15–16, 1875 [Philadelphia]. *Moonlight* (probably no. 162, as *On the Beach*)

1876 American Society of Painters in Water Colors, *Ninth Annual Exhibition*, January 31–February 26, 1876 [New York]. *Contraband* (no. 240)

The Century Association, April 1, 1876 [New York]. *Rooster* (probably no. 6)

1879 American Watercolor Society, *Twelfth Annual Exhibition*, February 3–March 1, 1879 [New York]. *The Pumpkin Patch* (as *Husking*), owner: The artist, purchased by Dr. Josiah Holland

1882 J. Eastman Chase, [*watercolors*], February 1882 [Boston]. *On the Cliff*

1883 American Watercolor Society, *Sixteenth Annual Exhibition*, January 29–February 25, 1883 [New York]. *Inside the Bar* (no. 272)

Doll & Richards, [*English and Maine Subjects*] December 1–15, 1883 [Boston]. *Homecoming* (no. 13, as *On the Way Home*)

1888 American Water Color Society, *Twenty-first Annual Exhibition*, January 30–February 25, 1888. *At Tampa, Florida* (no. 1, as *Tampa, Florida*)

1890 New York Athletic Club, *Fourth Annual Art Loan Exhibition*, March 1, 1890. *On the Cliff*

Union League Club, *Annual Loan Exhibition of Paintings in Water-Color*, April 10–12, 1890 [New York]. *On the Cliff* (no. 48, as *Sea View from the Cliffs*)

1892 New York Athletic Club, Sixth Annual Loan Exhibition Paintings Never before Exhibited, March 19, 1892. *Sponge Fishing, Bahamas* (no. 22), owner: Charles S. Homer Jr.

1893 Thomas B. Clarke [The Art House], *American Oil Paintings and Watercolors Loaned and For Sale. First Annual Summer Exhibition of the Art House*, exhibited at the Fifth Avenue Galleries, June 9 through August, 1893 [New York]. *On the Cliff* (no. 50, as *Children on the Cliffs*)

1895 Fifth Avenue Art Galleries, *Paintings by American Artists from Studios and Private Owners* [auction], March 8, 1895. *On the Cliff* (probably no. 59, as *Awaiting the Fishermen*)

1896 Fifth Avenue Art Galleries, *Paintings by American Artists* [auction], January 22, 1896. *Homecoming* (no. 55, as *The Return Home*)

1898 Union League Club, *The Paintings of Two Americans* [George Inness and Winslow Homer], March 10–October 1?, 1898 [New York]. *On the Cliff* (no. 44)

1899 American Art Association, *Private Art Collection of Thomas B. Clarke* [auction], February 7–18, 1899 [New York]. *On the Cliff* (probably no. 139, as *On the Cliffs*), purchased by Thomas L. Manson Jr.

Carnegie Institute, *Fourth Annual Exhibition*, November 2, 1899–January 1, 1900 [Pittsburgh]. *Watching the Breakers—A High Sea* (no. 120, as *High Seas*), owner: George G. Briggs

1900 Pennsylvania Academy of Fine Arts, *Sixty-ninth Annual Exhibition*, January 15, 1900–February 24, 1900 [Philadelphia]. *Watching the Breakers—A High Sea* (no. 26, as *High Seas*), owner: George G. Briggs

Society of American Artists, *Twenty-second Annual Exhibition*, March 24–April 28, 1900 [New York]. *Watching the Breakers—A High Sea* (no. 256, as *High Seas*), owner: George G. Briggs

1903 Boston Art Club, *Sixty-seventh Exhibition. Oil Paintings and Sculpture*, January 3–31, 1903. *Watching the Breakers—A High Sea* (no. 54, as *High Seas*), owner: George G. Briggs

Lotos Club, January 31, 1903 [New York]. *Homecoming* (no. 18, as *Maine Coast*)

1905 Lotos Club, *American Paintings from the Collection of John Harsen Rhoades*, opened December 23, 1905 [New York]. *Homecoming* (no. 32, as *Maine Coast*), owner: John Harsen Rhoades

1910 Philadelphia Water Color Club, *Eighth Annual Exhibition*, November 12–December 17, 1910. *Sailing Out of Gloucester* (no. 154)

1911 The Metropolitan Museum of Art, *Winslow Homer Memorial Exhibition: Loan Exhibition of Paintings by Winslow Homer*, February 6–March 19, 1911. *Watching the Breakers—A High Sea* (no. 17), owner: Mrs. Henry W. Rogers

Museum of Fine Arts, *Loan Exhibition of Paintings by Winslow Homer*, February 8–March 8, 1911 [Boston]. *Boy on Rocks* (as *Cliffs at Prout's Neck*)

Albright Art Gallery, *Sixth Annual Exhibition of Selected Paintings by American Artists*, May 12–August 28, 1911 [Buffalo]; traveled to City Art Museum of Saint Louis, September 17–November 17, 1911. *Watching the Breakers—A High Sea* (no. 70, as *Watching the Breakers: A High Sea*), owner: Mrs. H. W. Rogers

1915 The Museum of the Brooklyn Institute, *Water Colors by Winslow Homer*, October 16–November 7, 1915; traveled to The Century Association [New York], December 8, 1915–mid January 1916. *Moonlight* (no. 1), owner: Charles S. Homer. *At Tampa, Florida* (no. 59, as *Tampa, Two Flamingoes*), owner: Brooklyn Museum

1917 Museums of The Brooklyn Institute of Arts and Sciences, Department of Fine Art, 1917. *Sponge Fishing, Bahamas*, owner: Charles S. Homer. *Moonlight*, owner: Charles S. Homer

1921 Copley Society of Boston, *Paintings in Water Color by Winslow Homer, John S. Sargent, Dodge MacKnight*, March 5–22, 1921. *At Tampa, Florida* (no. 31, as *Two Flamingoes, Tampa*), owner: Brooklyn Museum

1923 Association Franco-Américaine d'Expositions de Peinture et de Sculpture, *Exposition d'Art Américain: John S. Sargent, R. A., Dodge MacKnight, Winslow Homer, Paul Manship*, May 18–June 25, 1923 [Paris]. *At Tampa, Florida* (no. 20), *Sponge Fishing, Bahamas* (no. 30)

Carnegie Institute, *Water Colors by Winslow Homer*, September 9–October 26, 1923. *At Tampa, Florida* (no. 4), *Sponge Fishing, Bahamas* (no. 41)

1930 The Museum of Modern Art, *Sixth Loan Exhibition: Winslow Homer, Albert P. Ryder, Thomas Eakins*, opened May 8, 1930. *Watching the Breakers: A High Sea* (no. 6)

1932 Macbeth Gallery, *Forty Years of American Art*, April 11–30, 1932. *Watching the Breakers—A High Sea* (no. 9)

1936 M. Knoedler & Co., *Winslow Homer 1836–1910: Loan Exhibition of Watercolors Commemorating the Centenary of his Birth*, January 20–February 8, 1936. *Sponge Fishing, Bahamas* (no. 26)

Pennsylvania Museum of Art, *Homer*, May 2–June 8, 1936. *Feeding the Chickens* (no. 1). *Watching the Breakers: A High Sea* (no. 24), owner: Canajoharie Art Gallery

Prout's Neck Association, *Century Loan Exhibition as a Memorial to Winslow Homer*, July 18–August 2, 1936 [Maine]. *Homework* (no. 2, as *Home Work*), owner: Mrs. Charles Savage Homer. *Woman on the Beach, Marshfield* (no. 10, as *On the Beach, Marshfield*), owner: Mrs. Charles Savage Homer. *Homecoming* (no. 26, as *Home-Coming*), owner: Bartlett Arkell. *Sponge Fishing, Bahamas* (no. 54), owner: Mrs. Charles Savage Homer. *Feeding the Chickens* (no. 56; may or may not be the painting currently owned by the Arkell Museum. The painting illustrated in the catalogue is *Farmyard Scene* now owned by the Sterling and Francine Clark Art Institute. The list of lenders to this exhibition does not include Arthur B. Homer, who then owned *Feeding the Chickens*. The exhibition catalogue found in Macbeth Gallery Records, Archives of American Art, also includes the handwritten notes "did not come" and "C L H Quincy" next to the entry for *Feeding the Chickens*.).

Whitney Museum of American Art, *Winslow Homer Centenary Exhibition*, December 15, 1936–January 15, 1937 [New York]. *Watching the Breakers—A High Sea* (no. 31, as *Watching the Breakers: A High Sea*), owner: Canajoharie Art Gallery

Macbeth Gallery, *An Introduction to Homer*, December 15, 1936–January 18, 1937 [New York]. *Woman on the Beach, Marshfield* (no. 42, as *On the Beach, Marshfield* "Mrs. Arthur B. Homer is the figure on the beach"), owner: Mr. Arthur P. Homer, esq. *Homework* (no. 43, as *Home Work*), *The Sea-Saw* (no. 47), owner: Canajoharie Art Gallery. *Sponge Fishing, Bahamas* (no. 57). *Feeding the Chickens* (no. 66, "Earliest known oil; date determined by apparent age of Arthur B. Homer, the boy in the picture.")

Carnegie Institute, *Centenary Exhibition of Works of Winslow Homer*, January 28–March 7, 1937 [Pittsburgh]. *Watching the Breakers—A High Sea* (no. 24), owner: Canajoharie Art Gallery. *Pumpkin Patch* (no. 77), owner: Ferargil, Inc. *At Tampa, Florida* (no. 91, as *Two Flamingoes, Tampa*), owner: Brooklyn Museums. *Sponge Fishing, Bahamas* (no. 112, as *Sponge Fishers, Bahamas*), owner: Mrs. Charles S. Homer. *Homecoming* (no. 121, as *Home-Coming*), owner: Bartlett Arkell.

FENIMORE ART MUSEUM

The Fenimore Art Museum, located on the shores of Otsego Lake—James Fenimore Cooper's "Glimmerglass"—in historic Cooperstown, New York, features a wide-ranging collection of American art including: folk art; important American 18th- and 19th-century landscape, genre, and portrait paintings; an extensive collection of domestic artifacts; more than 125,000 historical photographs representing the technical developments made in photography and providing extensive visual documentation of the region's unique history; and the renowned Eugene and Clare Thaw Collection of American Indian Art comprising more than 800 art objects representative of a broad geographic range of North American Indian cultures, from the Northwest Coast, Eastern Woodlands, Plains, Southwest, Great Lakes, and Prairie regions. The museum has also curated nationally recognized exhibitions featuring well-known American artists such as John Singer Sargent, Winslow Homer, Andrew Wyeth, Grandma Moses, and Edward Hopper. The Fenimore continues to develop new and insightful exhibitions season after season. **www.FenimoreArtMuseum.org**

THE ARKELL MUSEUM

The Arkell Museum's permanent collection includes works by leading American artists such as Gilbert Stuart, Winslow Homer, George Inness, Childe Hassam, William M. Chase, John Singer Sargent, Mary Cassatt, Maurice Prendergast, Robert Henri, Georgia O'Keeffe, Andrew Wyeth, and Thomas Hart Benton. Mohawk Valley history and Beech-Nut advertising are also featured in permanent and changing exhibitions. In 2007, the new museum building was added to the original Canajoharie Library and Art Gallery. The Arkell Museum is located halfway between Albany and Utica—just three blocks from exit 29 on the New York State Thruway (I-90). For information call 518-673-2314 or visit: **www.arkellmuseum.org**